FAMILY ADVENTURE GUIDE™

GEORGIA

"The Family Adventure Guide *series . . . enables parents to turn family travel into an exploration."*

—Alexandra Kennedy, Editor, *Family Fun*

FAMILY ADVENTURE GUIDE™ SERIES

GEORGIA

FAMILY ADVENTURE GUIDE™

by

CAROL THALIMER
with DAN THALIMER

A VOYAGER BOOK

The Globe Pequot Press

OLD SAYBROOK, CONNECTICUT

Photos © copyright Carol and Dan Thalimer
Cover and text design by Nancy Freeborn

Library of Congress Cataloging-in-Publication Data
Thalimer, Carol.
    Family adventure guide : Georgia / by Carol Thalimer with Dan Thalimer — 1st ed.
        p.   cm. — (Family adventure guide series)
    "A voyager book."
    Includes indexes.
    ISBN 1-56440-832-9
    1. Georgia—Guidebooks. 2. Family recreation—Georgia—Guidebooks.
    I. Thalimer, Dan. II. Title. III. Series.
F284.3.T485   1996
917.580453—dc20   95-45191
                                                                        CIP

Manufactured in the United States of America
First Edition/First Printing

To Chris and Tricia—*grand* traveling companions

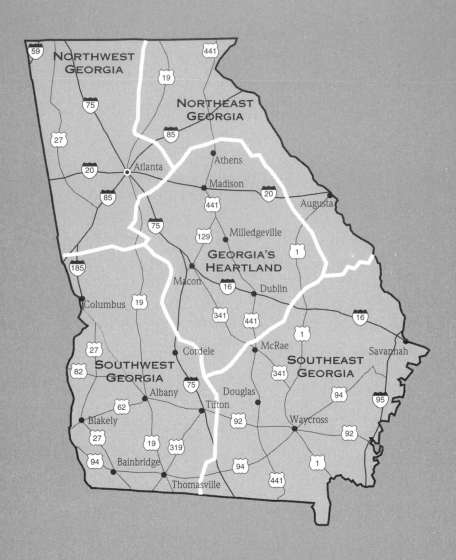

GEORGIA

NORTHWEST
GEORGIA

NORTHEAST
GEORGIA

Athens

Madison

Augusta

Milledgeville

GEORGIA'S
HEARTLAND

Macon

Dublin

Columbus

Cordele

McRae

Savannah

SOUTHWEST
GEORGIA

SOUTHEAST
GEORGIA

Albany

Douglas

Tifton

Waycross

Blakely

Bainbridge

Thomasville

Atlanta

CONTENTS

ACKNOWLEDGMENTS

A very special thanks to Elaine Hewett for serving as a research assistant on this and other projects. We also appreciate the assistance of Kathy Ansley of the Brunswick–Golden Isles Visitors Bureau; Jane Bozza, Kaufmann Associates; Sonia Eakins, Callaway Gardens Resort; Kitty Sikes, Georgia Department of Industry, Trade, and Tourism, Colonial Coast Region; and Jim Weidhaas, the Jekyll Island Authority.

INTRODUCTION

When we moved to Georgia in 1979, our four children ranged in age from ten to sixteen. In between school, scouts, church, band, drill team, cheerleading, soccer, and horse camp, we managed to visit some of our adopted state's wonderful sights, especially the northeast Georgia mountains and the beaches of the Golden Isles. Then we bought a travel agency, which rapidly expanded to three, and we spent several years exploring exotic destinations elsewhere. It wasn't until we sold the agencies and began writing about travel for several local newspapers and magazines that we started a serious campaign to discover what Georgia has to offer—especially in off-the-beaten-path locations. In our capacity as travel writers, we've combed the state to compile four other guides on traveling in the Peach State. Now our children are grown and on their own, and we have grandchildren to whom we can introduce the joys of traveling in Georgia. This past summer we investigated some of the state's marvelous family resort programs with seven-year-old Chris and four-year-old Tricia. We've been to a vast majority of the attractions listed in this guide, and the ones we haven't visited personally have been recommended by our friends at the state department of tourism, local chambers of commerce, or convention and visitors bureaus.

Although the state department of tourism divides the Peach State into nine regions, we decided it would be simpler for readers to begin exploring Georgia if we divided it into five regions: the Heartland, Northeast, Northwest, Southeast, and Southwest. The chapter for each region is introduced by a map that identifies the towns you will want to visit. The towns within each region are arranged from north to south and east to west so that you could actually start at the first town described and zigzag through the region, tracing a route all the way to the last town described. Some towns have only one special family-oriented attraction, some have several, and others boast dozens. For the most part, when there are only a few attractions to describe, we've listed them in alphabetical order unless it would make more sense to see a particular site first or if listing them alphabetically would require backtracking to see attractions that are located close together. In cities such as Atlanta and Savannah, we've clustered similar attractions together; such groups include museums, places to stay, places to eat, and so forth. Your family will be so enchanted with some of these places, you may never get to the next stop on the list. You will want to return to others again and again. We hope you and your family will enjoy exploring Georgia as much as we have with two generations of youngsters.

The prices and rates listed in this guidebook were confirmed at press time. We recommend, however, that you call establishments to obtain current information before traveling.

GEORGIA'S HEARTLAND

Although the abundant production of peaches in the heartland has given Georgia its nickname, the Peach State, the region may be better known for capturing the stereotypical antebellum southern way of life. In fact, so much of the area is suspended in the time prior to 1861 that it is frequently used as a location for period movies and television programs. In addition, the region is appealing to outdoor enthusiasts and shoppers. Seven state parks and historic sites, numerous lakes and rivers, and the Oconee National Forest offer camping, hiking, hunting, fishing, boating, picnicking, and golf, while quaint small-town shops vie with gigantic outlet malls for your purchasing dollar. Several trails crisscross the region, giving visitors a glimpse of different aspects of the heartland: the Antebellum Trail, which showcases a collection of pre–Civil War sites; the Antiques Trail, which connects some of the area's finest antiques shops; the Peach Blossom Trail, which highlights attractions pertaining to Georgia's peach-growing industry; and Treasures Between the Trails, which includes stops in small towns not included in the previous trails. For more information on the heartland or any of these trails, contact the Georgia Department of Industry, Trade, and Tourism at (404) 656–3590.

ATHENS

The Classic City, named for its counterpart in Greece, has been the home of the University of Georgia since it was chartered in 1785. A center of cul-

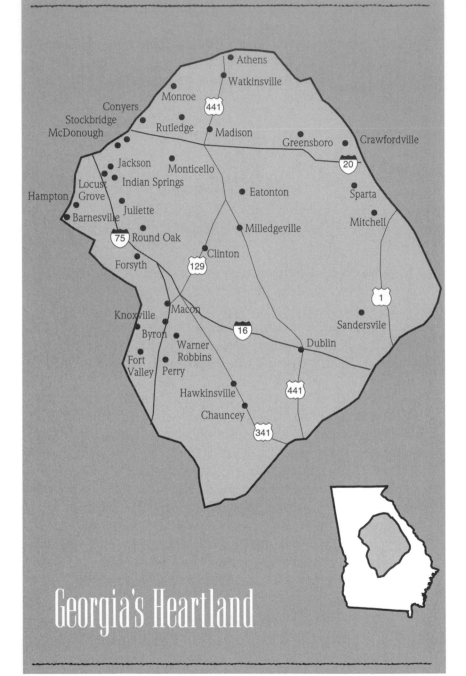

Georgia's Heartland

ture and wealth spared during the Civil War, Athens boasts dozens of Federal, Greek Revival, and Victorian homes.

Begin your tour of Athens by picking up information about the city's attractions at the **Church-Waddel-Brumby House/Welcome Center** at 280 East Dougherty Street. The Federal-style house, which is believed to be the oldest surviving residence in Athens, is open from 9:00 A.M. to 5:00 P.M. Monday through Saturday and from 2:00 to 5:00 P.M. on Sunday. To find out more, call (706) 546–1820.

At the **Butts-Mehre Heritage Museum** at Lumpkin and Pinecrest streets, sports enthusiasts of all ages enjoy the video displays, uniforms, playing equipment, trophies including two Heismans—photographs, and other memorabilia showcasing the outstanding athletic accomplishments of the University of Georgia's male and female athletes. The museum is open Monday through Friday from 8:00 A.M. to 5:00 P.M. and during home football games. For more information about the museum, call (706) 542–9094.

Children and adults are amazed by the one-of-a-kind **Double-Barreled Cannon** in Cannon Park on the City Hall lawn on Hancock Street. Developed as a prototype in 1863 during the Civil War, the artillery piece was designed to fire, simultaneously, two balls connected by a chain. Unfortunately, the device was spectacularly unsuccessful, so only one was built. The unique weapon survives undamaged and sits facing north—"just in case." It's always accessible. There's no phone.

Families relish wandering along the many wooded, flower-lined trails at the **State Botanical Garden of Georgia** at 2450 South Millidge Avenue. Located on 313 acres on the Middle Oconee River, the garden sports a large, modern conservatory/visitor center filled with tropical and semitropical plants as well as annuals of the season. The grounds are open daily from 8:00 A.M. to dusk. The conservatory is open Monday through Saturday from 9:00 A.M. to 4:30 P.M. and Sunday from 11:30 A.M. to 4:30 P.M. If the little ones are starving, you can grab a bite to eat at the Tea Room, which is open Monday through Friday from 11:00 A.M. to 2:00 P.M. and Saturday and Sunday from 11:30 A.M. to 2:30 P.M. To learn more about the gardens, call (706) 542–6151.

Children are surprised by the **Tree That Owns Itself** at the corner of Dearing and Finley streets. Athens is the only city we know of that has a tree that owns itself. This unusual situation came about in the late 1800s when Professor W. H. Jackson, who particularly enjoyed the shade of the tree, deeded it 8 feet of ground on all sides. It's alwasy accessible. There's no phone.

All ages of visitors marvel at the ship models, historical uniforms, Navy equipment, and galley gear at the **U.S. Navy Supply Corps Museum** at Prince and Oglethorpe avenues on the campus of the U.S. Navy Supply Corps School, where supply officers and personnel are trained to provide the items necessary for a modern navy to run smoothly. The museum is open Monday through Friday from 8:30 A.M. to 5:00 P.M.; it is closed weekends and federal holidays. To find out more, call (706) 354–7349.

WATKINSVILLE

South of Athens, family members can experience life in frontier Georgia by exploring the **Eagle Tavern Welcome Center** on US 441. During its colorful history the structure has served as a fort, a hotel, a stagecoach stop, and a store. One of the earliest surviving buildings in Oconee County, the tavern has been restored to its early Plain Style appearance—"two-up, two-down." Using simple furnishings from the 1700s, the downstairs replicates the tavern, in which, for the price of a drink, travelers could spread their bedrolls; the upstairs depicts the rooms available to stagecoach passengers. Other exhibits interpret the findings from several archaeological digs done on the property. The welcome center is open Monday through Friday from 9:00 A.M. to 5:00 P.M. and Sunday between 1:00 and 5:00 P.M. To learn more, call (706) 769–5197.

Not many of today's children have ever seen a covered bridge nor had the pleasure of walking or driving through one while enjoying the hollow sounds of the clattering floorboards. **Elder Mill Covered Bridge** on State 15 over Rose Creek offers families an opportunity to appreciate a bridge built in 1800. It is one of the last covered bridges still in use on a public road in Georgia.

Once a turn-of-the-century railroad depot, **Mockingbird Forge**, south on US 441 at the Farmington community, now houses the studios of several artisans. Children can watch a blacksmith, glass blower, potter, woodworker, and other crafters as they create handcrafted masterpieces. Hours vary, so it's best to call first rather than just dropping by. Call (706) 769–7147.

MONROE

You might want to tell your children why covered bridges were also known as kissing bridges. The sheltered spans were given this affectionate nickname because young couples could step into the privacy of the covered structure to catch a quick kiss out of sight of prying eyes.

Long before there were K-Marts and Wal-Marts folks visited general stores—as much to socialize and learn the latest news as they did to purchase goods. Families can re-create that time at the **Primitive Touch General Store** (136 North Broad Street), a museum of collectibles that captures the cheerful clutter of the old-time general store. Just a few of the 8,000 items that span the period from the 1800s to 1960 are old Coca-Cola machines, a wood-burning stove, antique wall phones, an old wooden washing machine, and much more. The store museum is open Tuesday through Saturday from 10:00 A.M. to 5:00 P.M. Call (770) 267–9799.

STOCKBRIDGE

A perfect place for a family outing, **Panola Mountain State Conservation Park** on State 155 offers 617 acres of hiking trails and wildlife specific to the Piedmont region. The most significant landmark is an awe-inspiring gigantic 100-acre granite monadnock, but other features that attract families to the park are guided hikes, an interpretive center, and picnicking areas. This park has seasonal hours, so it's best to check ahead. To learn more about the park, call (770) 389–7801.

CONYERS

All your family members will enjoy horsing around at the brand-new 1,400-acre **Georgia International Horse Park** on Gees Mill Road in Conyers, east of Stockbridge on I–20. Built to be the site of the 1996 Summer Olympic equestrian events as well as exciting periodic competitions like the National Barrel Horse Racing Super Show, dressage shows, and rodeos, the park also hosts fairs, craft shows, and musical concerts. To get a schedule of events, call (770) 785–6900.

Youngsters can get a glimpse into a religious life-style while parents enjoy the tranquility and beautiful old-world atmosphere at the

Monastery of Our Lady the Holy Spirit at 2625 State 212, 8 miles southwest of town. Visitors are welcome to participate in prayer services held at 7:00 A.M., 5:35 P.M., and 8:15 P.M., as well as Sunday Mass at 6:15 A.M. and 11:00 A.M. The greenhouse, which sells bonsai trees, is open Monday through Friday from 10:00 A.M. to noon and from 2:20 to 4:30 P.M., as well as Saturday from 10:00 A.M. to 4:30 P.M. The gift shop offers books, delicious homemade breads, and products from other monasteries around the country. It is open daily except Sunday from 9:30 A.M. to 4:30 P.M. You can enjoy the antics of the frolicking ducks while picnicking on the banks of the lovely pond. To learn more, call (770) 483–8705.

RUTLEDGE

Whether the family makes a day's outing or a week's vacation out of a visit to **Hard Labor Creek State Park,** 2 miles north of Rutledge off US 278, each family member will find plenty to do. The park offers cottages, golf, camping, fishing, a beach, boating, and horse stables and trails. Although the park maintains more than 17 miles of bridle trails, providing up to five hours of riding, it does not rent horses. For those who can BYOH (bring your own horse), stalls and trailer parking are available, as are campsites for the humans. Advance reservations for equestrian camping are required. The park is open daily from 7:00 A.M. to 10:00 P.M. To find out more about the facilities, call (706) 557–3001.

MADISON

Known as the city Sherman refused to burn, Madison had a reputation before the Civil War as "the most cultured and aristocratic town on the stage route from Charleston to New Orleans." A large portion of Madison's outstanding architecture was built between 1830 and 1860, but a significant number of Victorian structures from the late nineteenth century are also here. Designated by the U.S. Department of the Interior in 1974, the Madison Historic District was one of the first such districts in Georgia to be recognized and is still the largest designated historic area in the state.

Parents or grandparents can experience the nostalgia of their early school days at the **Madison-Morgan Cultural Center** (434 South Main

Street), where the original school bell still rings. Housed in an imposing 1895 Romanesque Revival school building, the structure served as one of the first graded schools in the South. The edifice must have seemed like a castle to children who had never before seen anything other than a one-room school, but even today's more sophisticated youngsters are sure to be impressed by the majestic structure as well. Currently the building houses authentically restored and furnished turn-of-the-century classrooms and a History Museum filled with nineteenth-century decorative arts, artifacts, and interpretive information about the Piedmont region of Georgia, as well as permanent and traveling art exhibits. Performances of the **Madison-Morgan Cultural Arts Festival** and other local, regional, national, and international groups are given in the apse-shaped auditorium, which still retains the original seats and chandelier. The cultural center is open Tuesday through Friday from 10:00 A.M. to 4:30 P.M. and Saturday and Sunday from 2:00 to 5:00 P.M. For more information and a schedule of events, call (706) 342–4743.

Families are surrounded by history at the **Morgan County African-American Museum** on Academy Street; it both preserves the African-American heritage and culture of the South and promotes an awareness of the contributions African-Americans have made to the area. The museum is open Tuesday through Friday from 10:00 A.M. to 4:00 P.M., Saturday from noon to 4:00 P.M., and Sunday by appointment. For more information, call (706) 342–9197.

Outdoor aficionados in the family can find something for every taste at 19,000-acre **Lake Oconee**, a Georgia Power lake that offers 235 miles of shoreline and swimming, fishing, waterskiing, and sailing. Several recreation areas provide campsites, beaches, docks, and/or restaurants. **Old Salem Park**, off State 44, has campsites with water and electrical hookups, showers, Laundromat, playground, picnic pavilion, beach, boat ramp, and dock. **Parks Ferry Park**, off State 44 or 278, has the same amenities as Old Salem Park. Call (706) 485–8704 for information on both. **Granite Shoals Marina**, off State 44, boasts a boat ramp, dry dock storage, restaurant, lodging, gasoline, boat repair, fishing supplies, and groceries. Call (770) 453–7639 to find out more about the marina. For more information about the lake in general, call the Lake Oconee Tourism and

Real Estate Council at (800) 886–5253.

The outstanding architectural treasures in Madison make excellent bed-and-breakfast inns. Several accept only adults as guests, but the following two welcome children. The **Brady Inn** at 250 North Second Street consists of two cozy, turn-of-the-century cottages connected and encircled by vast verandas. The inn operates a restaurant open for lunch as well as for dinner by reservation. To find out more or to make reservations, call (706) 342–4400. Typical of the two-story Federal-style construction of the Piedmont region, the 1830 slave-built **Burnett Place** at 317 Old Post Road is filled with a mix of traditional and contemporary furnishings and artwork. Some rooms feature working fireplaces. Call (706) 342–4034.

GREENSBORO

Indian artifacts, antique clothing, paintings, and a large photograph collection will intrigue the entire family at the **Greene County Historical Society Museum** on the corner of Greene and East streets downtown. The museum is open on Saturdays from 10:00 A.M. to noon or by appointment. To learn more, call (706) 453–7592.

Touring a historic jail when you know you can get out is always good family fun. Tour the **Olde Greene County "Gaol" Jail** on Green Street. Built in 1807, the rock jail with castellated battlements—one of the oldest penal institutions in Georgia—is patterned after the bastilles of the late eighteenth century. Tours are by appointment. To make arrangements, call (706) 453–7592.

Youngsters older than twelve are welcome at **The Davis House,** 106 North Laurel, a bed-and-breakfast that's a destination in itself. The stately red-brick mansion features spacious rooms with 14-foot ceilings and is furnished with comfortable antiques. The extensive grounds offer a swimming pool, tennis courts, lawn games, and horses. Call (706) 453–4213.

CRAWFORDVILLE

Families can find out more about the Civil War and a Georgia statesman at the **Alexander H. Stephens Home and Confederate Museum** on Park Street in Crawfordville, east of Greensboro on US 278. The antebellum home of the man who served as a U.S. senator, as vice president of the Confederacy, and as a governor of Georgia, the house and grounds are open for touring. Children enjoy learning about why Stephens called his home Liberty Hall. First, he felt that he was at liberty to do anything he pleased there. Second, any friend or even complete stranger could feel at liberty to spend the night at Stephens's home. In fact, Stephens had a special room built, which he called the Tramp's Room, to house travelers who needed a place to spend the night. Surrounding the house are Stephens's grave and several outbuildings, including a detached kitchen and a slave house. The adjacent Civil War Museum displays one of the best collections in the state of uniforms, weapons, medical equipment, documents, letters, and Civil War reunion souvenirs. Children are particularly fascinated by the life-size dioramas depicting scenes from the Civil War; these scenes include a family sending its sons off to war, soldiers in camp, and women at home supporting the war effort. The house and museum are open from 9:00 A.M. to 5:00 P.M. Tuesday through Saturday and Sunday from 2:00 to 5:30 P.M. They are closed Mondays, Thanksgiving, and Christmas. For more information, call (706) 456–2221.

Located on land behind the mansion, the **Alexander H. Stephens State Historic Park** is still within the city limits of Crawfordville. A pleasant place for a family to spend the day or even longer, the park boasts two lakes and offers tent, trailer, group, and pioneer camping, as well as fishing, boat rental, picnic pavilions, grills, and hiking trails. You might like to try the 6 mile Beaver Lodge Trail. The park is open daily from 7:00 A.M. to 10:00 P.M. To learn more, call (706) 456–2602.

Both the Alexander H. Stephens Home and the State Historic Park celebrate Christmas in a big way. The little ones' eyes will pop out when the park becomes a glittering fairyland of more than 120,000 sparkling lights, seventy displays, and 360 lighted Christmas trees. The observance, known as **Christmas in Dixie**, extends from Thanksgiving to New Year's Day. Call (706) 456–2455 for more information. **Christmas at Liberty Hall** features local citizens portraying Stephens and his friends as they welcome visitors to a candlelit celebration of music and refreshments. To find out more about the festivities, call (706) 456–2221.

SPARTA

Family adventure awaits at **Lake Sinclair,** which borders both Hancock and Putnam Counties and is accessible from State 16, south of I–20. The 75 miles of shoreline surrounding the lake feature restaurants, marinas, and accommodations ranging from primitive camping to luxurious condominiums. Several recreation areas and the lake itself provide boating, fishing, and hunting opportunities. To learn more, call (912) 452–4687 or (800) 693–1804.

EATONTON

The Uncle Remus/Br'er Rabbit stories have been children's favorites for almost one hundred years. Eatonton was the childhood home of journalist and author Joel Chandler Harris, who re-created the slave tales he had been told as a child. The small fry delight in the brightly dressed **Br'er Rabbit Statue** cavorting joyously on the courthouse lawn, and youngsters love the exhibits containing the "critters" at the nearby **Uncle Remus Museum and Park** on US 441. The museum is housed in a log cabin reminiscent of the slave cottage where Uncle Remus spun the yarns about the critters for the Little Boy. In addition to displays about plantation life, the museum contains Harris's personal memorabilia. The surrounding park contains plantation outbuildings and old-fashioned farm tools, as well as shady picnic areas and restrooms. Year-round the museum is open Monday and Wednesday through Saturdays from 10:00 to noon and from 1:00 to 5:00 P.M., as well as on Sunday from 2:00 to 5:00 P.M. During the summer, the park and museum are also open on Tuesday. To find out more, call (706) 485–6856.

One of the most ancient and unusual attractions in Georgia is the **Rock Eagle Effigy,** located on the grounds of the Rock Eagle 4-H Center on US 129/441. Youngsters are astonished by the gigantic stone figure of a prone bird measuring 102 feet from head to tail and 120 feet across the wingspan. The bird form is believed to have been built by Native Americans more than 6,000 years ago. Constructed entirely from quartz, the boulders are thought to have been brought from as far as 100 miles away without the benefit of horses or wheeled vehicles. Children are eager to climb the nearby tower that was constructed in the 1930s so the tumulus can be viewed from above. In addition, the park contains a 110-acre lake for boating and fishing activities, as well as shady picnic areas for a day of family fun. The park and the effigy are accessible during daylight hours. To learn more, call (706) 485–2831.

MONTICELLO

This small, gracious town, where the past is preserved for you to see, is the home of country music star Trisha Yearwood and is a stop on Treasures Between the Trails (see page 1). Step into the town's proud past by taking a walking tour of the Forsyth Street Historic District, where stately restored Southern antebellum and Victorian homes line the streets, which burst with dogwood blossoms in the spring. The buildings around the town square date from 1889 to 1906. A brochure describing the various buildings is available from the chamber of commerce at 115 East Green Street. To learn more about the town, call (706) 468–8994.

The **Oconee National Forest** is a wonderful place for families seeking adventure and variety. Encompassing 11,500 acres of public land, the forest includes the **Sinclair Recreational Area** on Lake Sinclair, two boat access recreational areas on Lake Oconee, and two wildlife management areas. Visiting the **Scull Shoals Historical Area** is a great way for children to learn about Georgia's past. The remains of a once-prosperous town, Georgia's first paper mill, a cotton gin, and a textile factory are reached by road or a 1-mile hiking trail. From there, the **Boarding House Trail** leads to the remains of an old boardinghouse, while the **Indian Mounds Trail** traverses the Oconee River floodplain to two prehistoric mounds. A truly fabulous place for a family to spend a day, the forest contains numerous hiking trails and five horseback riding trails that meander through the timberlands. Camping is permitted forest-wide. For more information, including *A Guide to the Chattahoochee-Oconee National Forests,* call (706) 468–2244.

JACKSON

Although caution is advised, family members have fun slipping and sliding as they clamber over the rocks while hiking to the top and bottom of the falls at **High Falls State Park** on High Falls Road off I–75. The southernmost falls in Georgia, High Falls marks the Piedmont Fall Line. With numerous campsites, a fishing lake (considered to be the best crappie lake in Georgia), boat rentals, a swimming pool, nature trails, and the magnificent falls themselves, this park is a perfect place for a family frolic. The park is open daily from 7:00 A.M. to 10:00 P.M. To learn more, call (912) 994–5080.

Busy **Jackson Lake,** 5 miles northeast of Jackson, is a 4,700-acre impoundment with 135 miles of shoreline providing fun for all ages with many opportunities for swimming, fishing, and boating. Because it's not very deep, the lake is warmer than others in the area, making it particularly popular with swimmers. The reservoir, which sports six marinas and several restaurants, is easily accessible from I–75 by taking State 16 or from I–20 via State 36. For more information, call (770) 775–4753.

INDIAN SPRINGS

A good place for families to experience activities together is at the **Dauset Trails Nature Center**, located on 1,000 acres on Mount Vernon Road off State 42. In addition to hiking the 6 miles of nature trails, you should check for scheduled programs about ecology issues and plant, tree, and wildlife identification. The center is open from 9:00 A.M. to 5:00 P.M. except Sunday, when the hours are noon to 5:00 P.M. Call (770) 775–6798 to learn more.

You'll have the feeling that you've gone back a century and a half at the historic **Indian Springs Hotel** (on State Highway 42), built in 1823 by Chief William McIntosh, leader of the Lower Creek Nation. Furnished in pieces appropriate to the period, the downstairs depicts a tavern; upstairs are period bedrooms. Open for tours during special events that occur about every other month, the hotel is surrounded by the only authentic nineteenth-century flower and herb garden in the Southeast. Sure to excite the youngsters' imaginations, the premier annual event is the September **Indian Festival** that features authentic circle dances, handmade Native American crafts, and demonstrations of such skills as tanning hides, drum and flute making, and woodworking. Other events include a November **Civil War Reenactment,** a December **Christmas Bazaar,** a March **Quilt and Antique Car Show,** an April **Scottish Festival,** and a May **Plant Sale** from the garden. To learn more or to get a schedule of events, call (770) 775–2493.

Named for the medicinal spring that people still use today, **Indian Springs State Park** on State 42 is the oldest state park in the nation. People come here daily to collect the medicinal spring water. A great place to relax for a day or longer, the park's facilities and activities include a lake with a beach, fishing, boat rentals, tent and trailer sites, cottages, picnicking, and nature trails. On the park grounds is the quaint 1890 **Indian Springs Chapel,** often used for weddings. The park is open daily from 7:00 A.M. to 10:00 P.M. For information on the park, call (770) 775–7241. To find out more about the chapel, call (770) 775–2493.

LOCUST GROVE

Turn your children loose at **B & H Orchards** at 381 Davis Lake Road, where all of you can pick your own succulent Georgia peaches. Fresh fruit from the hundreds of trees is available from June through August. For more information, call (770) 957–4330.

Folks of all ages have a good time around animals. A real blessing to injured creatures, **Noah's Ark Animal Rehabilitation Center** at 1425 Locust Grove Road off State 42 ministers to more than 600 at last count. Everyone in the family finds an animal that is sure to enchant him or her. The center also provides periodic educational programs. Be sure to bring your camera; pictures of children and animals are always guaranteed to create precious memories. The center is open on Fridays and Saturdays from noon to 5:00 P.M. and on Tuesdays and Thursdays by appointment. To learn more about Noah's Ark, call (770) 957–0888.

MCDONOUGH

Another outstanding place for those who love animals is the newly constructed **Tamingo Farms Equestrian Center** at 108 Peach Drive. Not only does the center offer rentals and lessons, but the 10,000-seat arena hosts hunter, jumper, and dressage shows, as well as two rodeos annually. For more information about rentals and lessons or for a schedule of events, call (770) 957–RIDE/7433.

Take a look at the past at The **Turner Hunt Clemmons Cabin** on State Highway 20 east of the city. Built in 1832 with wooden pegs, it is the oldest structure in Henry County. Open by appointment. For more information or an appointment, call the Henry County Convention and Visitors Bureau at (770) 957–5786 from 9:00 A.M. to 5:00 P.M. Monday through Friday.

HAMPTON

Something exciting is always happening at the **Atlanta Motor Speedway** on US 19/41S. It hosts two NASCAR Winston Cup races and the Busch Grand National, as well as several IMSA and ARCA events. For a schedule of events for the March through November season, call (770) 946–4211.

BARNESVILLE

Early in this century, small Barnesville was the home of four buggy manufacturing factories, earning the town the title "Buggy Capital of the World." Although all the factories are gone, the hamlet still celebrates its heritage with **Barnesville Buggy Days**, the third weekend of September. Let your family experience the days of spoke wheels and surrey tops by participating in this celebration that includes a decorated buggy parade, arts and crafts, antiques, and buggy rides. For more information about the festival, contact the Barnesville-Lamar County chamber of commerce at (770) 358–2732.

FORSYTH

Forsyth is brilliant with yellow forsythias each spring. To celebrate the cheery, lemon-colored blossoms, the town sponsors an annual **Forsythia Festival** in April. If your family likes festivals, you can relax at this one for a day of arts and crafts, a 5K run, a street dance, a parade, sporting events, a horse show, food booths, and children's activities. For more information, call (912) 994–9239.

If you have bird-watchers in your family, you'll enjoy a visit to the **Rum Creek Wildlife Management Area,** located 7 miles east of town on State 18. An 18,000-acre habitat with one of the most varied bird populations in the Southeast, the preserve is open from sunrise to sunset except during hunting season, when the area is open only to hunters. To learn more, call (912) 994–2439.

A visit to the **Whistle Stop Museum**, located in an 1899 Victorian railroad depot just off I-75, will foster your children's interest in the past. Examine local artifacts that span the period from pre-colonization to the twentieth century. One of the highlights is the desk *Uncle Remus* author Joel Chandler Harris used when he was a reporter for the Monroe *Advertiser.* The museum is open Tuesday through Friday from 10:00 A.M. to 5:00 P.M. and Saturday from 10:00 A.M. to 1:00 P.M. For more information, call (912) 994–7030.

JULIETTE

You'll recognize quaint, tiny, one-street Juliette as the film location of the movie *Fried Green Tomatoes.* The turn-of-the-century depot, shops, bank, drugstore, and other buildings along McCrackin Street have been resurrected as antique shops, gift and clothing boutiques, and eateries. Across the railroad tracks on the banks of **Lake Juliette** is the dejected skeleton of the **Juliette Grist Mill**, at one time the world's largest water-powered grist mill. Plans call for it to be transformed into more shops and eateries. On a hot day family members will enjoy a splash in **Lake Juliette**, a 3,600-acre recreation lake with 62 miles of shoreline providing plenty of opportunities for water sports. To find out about recreational activities, call (912) 994–0022.

What most folks come to Juliette for, however, is to sit down amidst the memorabilia left from the movie set for a plentiful repast of Southern home cookin' specialties, including the famous fried green tomatoes, at the **Whistle Stop Café** on McCrackin Street. The café is open Monday through Saturday from 8:00 A.M. to 2:00 P.M. and Sunday from noon to 7:00 P.M. on a first-come, first-served basis. Just sign your name to the list hanging on the screen door and you'll be called when it's your turn. More than likely there will be a line, but you can pass the wait rocking in one of the chairs on the front porch. Call (912) 994–3670.

For an activity both educational and historical for all family members, examine the farm life represented at **Jarrell Plantation Historic Site** on Jarrell Plantation Road 8 miles southeast of Juliette. The Jarrell family lived on the farm from the 1840s to the 1940s, after which they donated all the buildings and their contents to the state—the most complete original family collection of artifacts in Georgia. Although most folks tend to think of

Fans of the movie Fried Green Tomatoes *will enjoy visiting the Whistle Stop Cafe, which was featured in that film.*

Tara in the context of plantation life, this one was simply a self-contained farm complex that allowed family members to produce almost everything they needed. The site includes several simple houses filled with primitive furniture and everyday necessities such as spinning wheels and looms. Children are even more fascinated by the sawmill, carpenter shop, blacksmith shop, and several beehives and wheat houses, as well as by the farm tools and machinery, such as a cane furnace, steam-powered cotton gin, gristmill, sawmill, and a shingle mill. A barn, farm animals, a grape arbor, and a garden lend an air of authenticity. You'll need to spend considerable time here to explore all the farm's offerings. Special events pertaining to farm life occur throughout the year. The historic site is open Tuesday through Saturday from 9:00 A.M. to 5:00 P.M. and Sunday from 2:00 to 5:30 P.M. It is closed on Thanksgiving and Christmas. For more information and a schedule of special events, call (912) 986–5172.

ROUND OAK

The town was named for a huge ancient oak where Native Americans once held powwows. Families seeking a quiet getaway can spend some time in the nearby 35,000-acre **Piedmont National Wildlife Refuge** in Round Oak on Juliette Road. A sanctuary for the endangered red-cockaded woodpecker and other birds, the refuge's interpretive trails are especially popular with bird-watchers. In addition, there is a visitor center and a fishing pond exclusively for children. Hunting for deer, turkey, and small game is also permitted in season. The refuge is open from dawn to dusk daily from May 1 through September 3; the visitor center is open Monday through Friday from 8:00 A.M. to 4:30 P.M. and Saturday and Sunday from 9:00 A.M. to 5:30 P.M. For hunting and fishing regulations and other information, call (912) 986-5441.

MILLEDGEVILLE

Milledgeville served as Georgia's capital from 1804 to 1868, a period that included the momentous Civil War years. Filled with historic buildings from that era, the town is considered to be the only surviving example of a complete federal-period city. Always a favorite with children, a **Trolley Tour** of Milledgeville's historic district should definitely be the first activity on the itinerary of any family visiting the small town. Originating at the Milledgeville Tourism and Trade Office (200 West Hancock Street), the public tours run Tuesday and Friday at 10:00 A.M. except on holidays; group tours can be arranged by appointment. To find out more, call (912) 452 4687 or (800) 653-1804.

Always a popular family diversion, the **Brown's Crossing Craftsman Fair** in April and October is the area's premier festival, consistently listed among the top twenty events in the Southeast by the Southeast Tourism Society, as well as in the top 200 expositions in the country by the National Tour Bus Association. In addition to food, music, and other activities, highlights of the fair include demonstrations of the skills of yesteryear and sales of crafts. The fair's location (400 Brown's Crossing Road) was formerly a busy cotton ginning center. For more information, call (912) 452-9327.

If your family loves the outdoors, they'll appreciate a visit to the fifty-acre **Lockerly Arboretum** on US 441. You can explore nature trails, a spring-fed pond, and an artesian well, or you can participate in a plant identification program. The arboretum is open Monday through Friday from 8:30 A.M. to 4:30 P.M., and Saturday from 1:00 to 5:00 P.M. during standard time and 10:00 A.M. to 2:00 P.M. during daylight savings time. Call (912) 452–2112.

Youngsters will find plenty to do at the **Old Capital Celebration**, held the third weekend in April. Among the activities are games, dances, road races, sporting events, crafts, food, music, and more. The adults can partake of fashion shows, tours of homes and gardens, and cultural activities. To find out more about the festival, call the Tourism and Trade office at (912) 452–4687.

Young people older than twelve are welcome as guests at **Mara's Tara**, 330 West Greene Street. A beautiful Greek Revival mansion built in 1825, it now operates as a bed-and-breakfast. For more information or reservations, call (912) 453–2732.

MITCHELL

History and outdoor fun await families who visit **Hamburg State Park** on State 248. In addition to a historic gristmill and a country museum, families will find tent and trailer sites, picnicking facilities, a lake, fishing, a boat ramp, and canoe and pedal boat rentals, as well as nature and hiking trails. A family favorite, the **Hamburg Harvest Festival** is an annual event at the park. The park is open from 7 A.M. to 10:00 P.M. daily. For more information, call (912) 552–2393.

SANDERSVILLE

Kaolin, a white clay product known in these parts as white gold, is Georgia's largest export product, even though most people have never heard of it. Primarily used in making porcelain, kaolin is also an ingredient in some medicines and cosmetics and is used as a filler in textiles, paper, and rubber. You can tour a kaolin quarry and processing plant by making advance reservations. Call for more information. The **Kaolin Festival** is a week-long arts and crafts festival beginning the first Saturday in October and culminating with a parade on the second Saturday. To find out more about the festival, call (912) 552–3288.

CLINTON

Take a trip back in time and see what life in central Georgia was like almost 200 years ago when Clinton was a bustling early nineteenth-century county seat. Because early settlers were from New England, the town's plan, architecture, and location of the houses resemble those of the northeastern United States. Despite the Civil War and other catastrophes, twelve houses and a church built between 1808 and 1830 survive. Special events throughout the year will foster your children's interest in the past of this tiny town. **Clinton's War Days** is an April Civil War reenactment. A fall quilt show and a **Christmas Tour of Homes** are also on the schedule. **Old Clinton Roadside Park** on US 129 is a wooded area with huge granite outcroppings marking the Piedmont Fall Line. It's an excellent place to savor a family picnic. For more information about Clinton, call the Macon-Bibb County Convention and Visitors Bureau at (912) 743–3401.

MACON

Macon, one of the most gracious cities in Georgia, is known as the City of White Columns and Cherry Blossoms because of its profusion of antebellum mansions and the fact that it has more cherry trees than Washington, D.C. Spared during the Civil War, the city therefore showcases several significant antebellum structures. The 200,000 Yoshino cherry trees were a gift from the Japanese government. To get an overview of the city, take a horse-and-carriage or van tour of Macon's historic districts with **Sidney's Old South Historic Tours,** which departs from the **Macon-Bibb County Convention and Visitors Bureau/Welcome Center** housed in the magnificent, restored **Terminal Station** at 200 Cherry Street. Tours are conducted Monday through Saturday from 10:00 A.M. to 2:00 P.M. or by appointment. When you return to the welcome center, get tour, lodging, restaurant, and other information from the friendly staff members or volunteers who can answer any questions your family might have. To find out more about the tours or the welcome center, call (912) 743–3401.

The **Georgia Music Hall of Fame**, adjacent to Terminal Station at Martin Luther King, Jr. Boulevard and Mulberry Street, focuses on Georgia's diverse musical heritage through music and memorabilia from Georgia artists such as Macon natives Otis Redding, Little Richard

Penniman, Lena Horne, and the Allman Brothers, as well as Georgia greats James Brown, R. E. M., the B–52s, and Columbus's "Mother of the Blues"—Gertrude "Ma" Rainey. Vintage listening rooms, each devoted to a different style of music, feature memorabilia and artifacts representative of that type of music. An audio program intermixes music, artists' interviews, and historical context. The finale is an extravaganza of music, lights, and video in the Starlight Theater. To find out more about the museum, call (912) 743–3401 or (800) 768–3401.

Expose your youngsters to African-American history and culture at the **Harriet Tubman Museum**, 340 Walnut Street, named for the Macon native who created the underground railroad that helped slaves escape to the North prior to and during the Civil War. Artifacts and art in the seven galleries trace the achievements of African-Americans from slavery through the present. The museum is open Monday through Friday from 10:00 A.M. to 5:00 P.M., Saturday from 2:00 to 5:00 P.M., and Sunday from 2:00 to 6:00 P.M. For more information, call (912) 743–8544.

More than 400 enticing family-oriented events, including music, entertainment, arts and crafts, and a variety of food, draw visitors to the **Macon Cherry Blossom Festival** held each March amid the blossoming of the city's cherry trees. The city's most popular annual event, the fair celebrates the city's history, beauty, and hospitality. Call (912) 751–7429.

Satisfy the children's curiosity about the heavens with a visit to the **Mark Smith Planetarium** (4182 Forsyth Road), which is part of the **Museum of Arts and Sciences**. Various scientific programs are conducted Monday through Thursday and Saturday from 9:00 A.M. to 5:00 P.M. Planetary presentations are given daily in the observatory at 4:00 P.M. Additional shows are offered on weekends. On Friday evenings at 7:00 P.M., the *Sky Over Macon* program showcases the night sky. To learn more about the programs offered at the planetarium, call (912) 477–3232. In addition to the planetarium, the Museum of Arts and Sciences features exhibits, programs, and live animal shows—all of which captivate all ages. Children are awed by the 40 million-year-old whale fossil discovered near Macon. After exploring all the displays, if you have any energy left, stroll through the nature trails on the property. The museum is open Monday through Saturday from 9:00 A.M. to 5:00 P.M., with extended hours on

Friday until 9:00 P.M., as well as on Sunday from 1:00 to 5:00 P.M. To find out more, call (912) 477-3232.

A visit to the **Ocmulgee National Monument** (1207 Emory Highway) provides your children with an excellent lesson in history and archaeology. At the 683-acre site you can examine 12,000 years of human habitation in the Southeast. A succession of Native American cultures is documented, but the major concentration is on the Mississippian civilization that flourished here from A.D. 900 to 1100. Several Indian mounds include temple and funeral knolls. Exhibits, designed to kindle children's inquisitiveness and spark their imaginations, include an archaeologically recreated ceremonial earthlodge, a museum, and a movie called *People of the Macon Plateau*. Several nature trails wind through the site as well. The historic site is open daily from 9:00 A.M. to 5:00 P.M. except on Christmas and New Year's Day. For more information or a schedule of special weekend events, call (912) 752-8257.

Just imagine how captivated your youngsters will be when they see the Yankee cannonball still embedded in the parlor of the **Old Cannonball House and Confederate Museum** at 856 Mulberry Street. The 1853 Greek Revival mansion was the only structure in the city hit during an 1864 attack on the city. The house and museum, which contain Civil War artifacts, are open Tuesday through Friday from 10:00 A.M. to 1:00 P.M. and 2:00 to 4:00 P.M. as well as on Saturday and Sunday from 1:30 to 4:30 P.M. To learn more, call (912) 475-5982.

The family can become better acquainted with Macon's black musical heritage by taking a walking or driving tour of the **Pleasant Hill Historic District**, one of the first black neighborhoods listed on the National Register of Historic Places. The community was the home of musical greats Otis Redding, Little Richard Penniman, and Lena Horne. Macon's WIBB-AM is where James Brown got his break, and the historic **Douglass Theater** hosted Bessie Smith, Cab Calloway, and Count Basie. The Pleasant Hill neighborhood is always accessible. Call the convention and visitors bureau at (912) 743-3401.

Leave the hustle and bustle of the city behind with a visit to the **Tobesofkee Recreation Area** (6600 Mosley Dixon Road) on **Lake Tobesofkee**. It offers two campgrounds with tent and trailer sites, swimming, boating, fishing, picnicking, a playground, a water slide, tennis, softball, a marina, a horse show ring, and four parks with beaches. The recreation area is open from 6:00 A.M. to 10:00 P.M. daily. To learn more about the park, call (912) 474–8770.

Your family can visualize what an Old South Christmas celebration must have been like during Macon's **White Columns and Holly,** a month-long celebration that features concerts, theater productions, tours of homes, crafts and baked goods sales, and much more. For more information, call (912) 743–3401.

While visiting Macon, you can also get a taste of the past by staying in the lap of luxury at the **1842 Inn** at 353 College Street. Conveniently located for touring Macon's historic neighborhoods, the antebellum Greek Revival main house and its Victorian cottage provide opulent accommodations. For more information, call (912) 741–1842.

KNOXVILLE

Knoxville is noted as the birthplace of John Stith Pemberton, creator of the Coca-Cola formula, the site of the state's oldest continuously used courthouse. Memorabilia and documents pertaining to local history are on display at the **Old Knoxville Jail and Museum,** built in 1834. It is open on Saturday from 10:00 A.M. to noon and Sunday from 3:00 to 5:00 P.M. For more information, call (912) 836–3825.

FORT VALLEY

Fort Valley is the county seat of Peach County, the heart of peach growing and peach packing in Georgia. During the summer peach season, your family can tour some of the packing plants, buy fresh peaches from numerous stands along the roadside, or experience the fun of picking your own. For more information about touring the plants, call (912) 825–3733. Food—especially anything containing juicy peaches—is the highlight of the **June Peach Festival,** a salute to the lifeblood of the region, but arts and crafts and entertainment also figure prominently in the family-oriented festivities. To find out more, call (912) 825–4002.

Children are amazed to learn that the **Blue Bird Body Company**

(North Camellia Boulevard) is the largest manufacturer of school buses in the world, while parents are interested to find out that the company also produces the Wanderlodge, an exclusive luxury recreational vehicle. Here's your chance to watch both vehicles being made. Tours of the plant are available by appointment. Call (912) 825–2021 for more information.

Families can gain an appreciation of what is involved in getting peaches from the orchard to the grocery store by touring the **Lane Packing Company** on State 96. During the summer peach season you can watch 300,000 peaches per hour being individually weighed, counted, separated, and packed using computer-controlled equipment and soft-handling techniques. While you're there, visit the gift shop and be sure to try the homemade peach ice cream or the peach or blueberry cobbler. To find out about tours, call (912) 825–9227.

For a different family outing, make a stop at the historic **Massee Lane Gardens** (One Massee Lane off State 49), the headquarters of the American Camellia Society. Acres of pink, red, white, and varicolored camellias bloom from fall through spring; other brilliant flowers blossom throughout the year. The complex also includes two museums, one containing an extensive collection of Boehm porcelains. Because the camellia season is in the winter, the grounds and museums are open from November through March from 9:00 A.M. to 5:00 P.M. and on Sunday from 1:00 to 5:00 P.M. The remainder of the year they are open Monday through Friday from 9:00 A.M. to 5:00 P.M. There's no charge for children younger than twelve. To learn more, call (912) 967–2358 or 967–2722.

Pecans are another Georgia specialty that you'll want to take home from a family getaway. The **Jolly Nut Company**, 100 Commercial Drive, is a quaint, historical shop chock-full of products such as candies, cakes, and pies made from the tasty nut. Other Georgia products and gifts are also sold here. The store is open Monday through Friday from 9:00 A.M. to 5:00 P.M.. During the fall harvest season, it is also open on Saturdays from 9:00 A.M. to 5:00 P.M. For more information, call (912) 825–7733 or (800) 332–1505.

Families with children older than ten will enjoy a stay at the **Evans-Cantrell House** (300 College Street), a mansion built in 1916 by Georgia's Peach King and now operating as a bed-and-breakfast. To find out more, call (912) 825–0611.

BYRON

Although Georgia has slipped to third place in peach production, it is still known as the Peach State. Children are dazzled by the **Big Peach Monument,** which honors the delectable fruit. Located at the Peach Festival Outlet Center (311 State 49N), it is one of the most-photographed landmarks in the state. It's always accessible. The telephone number of the outlet center is (912) 956–1855.

Families can relive the glory days of the railroads at the restored 1870s **Byron Depot** (101 Murdock Lane). Examine the extensive collection of photographs and a variety of railroad memorabilia. Call (912) 956–3600 to arrange a tour.

PERRY

During May and June, young ones can feast their eyes on strolling peacocks and more than 1,000 colorful varieties of lilies at **Cranshaw's One Horse Farm and Day Lily Garden** on Sandefur Road off US 41. The grounds are open from sunup to sundown and make an ideal place to spread out a picnic. For more information, call (912) 987–3268.

A ten-day October extravaganza, the **Georgia National Fair,** held on the Georgia National Fairgrounds at I–75 and US 41, is a family-oriented festival featuring livestock events, horse shows, youth exhibits, home and fine arts competitions, concerts, entertainment, a midway, a circus, food, and fireworks. For more information, call (912) 987–3247 or call (800) YUR–FAIR within Georgia.

The **Georgia National Fairgrounds and Agricenter** is in itself a mammoth exhibition facility that not only serves as the home of the Georgia National Fair, but also as a venue for stock shows, rodeos, and numerous special events throughout the year that attract families in search of adventure. The **Southeastern Antiques and Collectibles Market** is held at the fairgrounds on the fourth weekend of each month. To find out more or for a schedule of events, call (912) 987–2774.

Held in both April and October, the award-winning **Mossy Creek Barnyard Festival** features pioneer demonstrations that permit families to get a glimpse into "The Way It Used to Be." In addition, the popular fair features music, arts and crafts, and plenty of family fun. To find the festival, take exit 44 off I–75 and travel 6 miles east on State 96. For more information, call (912) 922–8265.

During the mid-May to mid-August peach season, orchards along US 41 north of the city invite visitors to pick their own peaches or buy them from numerous roadside stands. Allow your children the pleasure of picking some of the juicy fruit. They may agree with adults that the peaches you pick yourself taste the best.

WARNER ROBINS

Warner Robins is Georgia's sixth largest city and is the home of Robins Air Force Base. The fun begins at the **Museum of Aviation** (State 247 and Russell Parkway), the fastest-growing military aviation museum in the Southeast. Energetic children can alternate between both indoor and outdoor exhibits at the forty-five-acre site. Youngsters can imagine the thrill of piloting one of the eighty-five historic aircraft, such as the F-15A from Desert Storm. The **Georgia Aviation Hall of Fame,** housed at the museum, was created by the Georgia General Assembly to honor living and dead Georgia military and civilian aviators. The museum and hall of fame are open from 10:00 A.M. to 5:00 P.M. daily. To learn more, call (912) 926–6870/4242.

DUBLIN

Get a taste of the past at **Chappell's Mill,** 13 miles north of Dublin on US 441. Built in 1811, the mill is still in operation using the old process of dry milling to grind more than 15,000 bushels of grain a year. Children can watch the grinding operation Monday through Friday from 8:00 A.M. to 5:00 P.M. For more information, call (912) 272–5128.

The **Dublin-Laurens St. Patrick's Day Festival,** a lavish two-week salute to Irish ancestry, is the second-largest St. Paddy's celebration in the state. Every year the town is blanketed in green as it welcomes 25,000 to 30,000 visitors to events ranging from a leprechaun contest to cooking the world's largest pot of Irish stew. Super Weekend—the weekend of St. Patrick's Day or the one immediately following it if the holiday falls during the week—is crammed with activities such as beauty pageants, a parade, hot air balloons, road races, and square dancing. To get in on the fun, call (912) 272–1822.

Although it's only a once-a-year occurrence, if you're in the Dublin area on the last Thursday in July, participate in a **Farm Tour of Laurens County.** Children can learn about farm operations, traditional crops, and sheep herding dogs. Transportation and lunch are included. Call the Laurens County Extension Service at (912) 272–2277 for more information or reservations.

Let your children see how early Native Americans trapped fish at the **Fish Trap Cut** on State 19. Believed to have been built on the Oconee River between 1000 B.C. and A.D. 1500, the cut was used as an aboriginal fish trap. In addition, you can explore a large rectangular mound, a smaller round mound, and a canal that survive from the same period. The site is always accessible. There's no phone. While you're in the area, pack a picnic to savor on the sandy shores of the Oconee River or take an inner tube or raft in which to float down the river. A pleasant place from which to watch others floating by is **Riverwalk Park,** north of town on US 319.

Small, shady **Stubbs Park,** North Drive, is a gathering point for fairs and festivals. Active families can take advantage of the tennis and basketball courts, picnic shelters, and a playground. Always accessible. For more information, call (912) 272–1620.

CHAUNCEY

Filled with mineral waters from a natural spring, **Jay Bird Springs**, located 12 miles south of Eastman on US 341S, is the oldest public swimming pool in Georgia. Diversions suitable to children of all ages include a 150-foot water slide; miniature golf; train rides; a game room with pool tables, air hockey, and video games; and a skating rink. A pleasant place for families to stay while touring the immediate area, the complex also features a restaurant, cabins, a motel, campsites, a country store, and a picnic area. The amusements are open from 4:00 to 8:00 P.M. on weekdays; the pool is open from 10:00 A.M. to 8:00 P.M. on weekends; and the skating rink is open until 11:00 P.M. on weekends. For more information, call (912) 868–2728.

HAWKINSVILLE

Hawkinsville is best known for harness training and racing and, in fact, is known as the Harness Horse Training Capital of the South. Standardbred horses, which are either pacers or trotters, as well as their drivers and trainers are headquartered in Hawkinsville from fall through April. A superb family outing is a visit to the **Hawkinsville Harness Horse Training Facility**, US 129, to watch the magnificent Standardbreds at work pulling sulkies around the track and at rest in their stalls. The best time to see the horses gliding around the half-mile and mile-long red clay tracks is early in the morning, but you can wander around the dozen stables and visit with the horses, trainers, and drivers anytime. To learn more, call (912) 892–9463.

Just before the horses return to the North and begin their spring through fall racing circuit, they have a trial run—a racing event that attracts spectators from all over Georgia and the Southeast. A special treat for families, the **Hawkinsville Harness Festival**, held in early April, features two days of races, as well as arts and crafts, food booths, a barbecue cook-off, musical entertainment, and historic home tours. For more information, call the Hawkinsville-Pulaski chamber of commerce at (912) 783–1717.

A fruit you might never expect to be grown in Georgia is the kiwi, native to New Zealand. **Double Q Farms**, 1475 State 26, has been growing the tart green produce successfully since 1986 and is now the state's largest grower. The last weekend in October the family can make an afternoon out of picking its own kiwi to take home. From October through April, you can purchase kiwi jams and other fruit and fruit products at the farm store from 8:00 A.M. to 5:00 P.M., but it's best to call ahead to make sure someone is there. The store is closed the remainder of the year. For more information, call (912) 892–3794.

You and the children can buy pecan candy and other pecan products at the **Nut House in the Grove** gift shop, an outlet of **Gooseneck Farms**, a prime producer of pecans. Located on Abbeville Highway, the shop is open 9:00 A.M. to 5:00 P.M. Monday through Saturday from Labor Day to Memorial Day. It is closed during the summer. To find out more, call (912) 783–1063 or (800) 537–6965.

Harness racing enthusiasts won't want to miss the Hawkinsville Harness Festival held in early April in Hawkinsville.

For even more family adventure, the **Ocmulgee River,** conveniently located just south of the downtown district, offers excellent fishing and a public boat landing. The nearby **Ocmulgee Wildlife Management Area** provides family opportunities for hunting, fishing, camping, water skiing, and boating. Wildlife management areas are open for the various activities twenty-four hours a day except during hunting season when other activities are prohibited. For more information, call the Georgia Department of Natural Resources at (404) 535–5700.

NORTHEAST GEORGIA

For more than 100 years tourists have flocked to Georgia's northern mountains to escape the heat of the lowlands as well as the hustle and bustle of city life. Folks used to come by train and stay for weeks. Now visitors arrive by car and may stay as little as a day or as long as the entire summer. Some never leave. The pollution-free air and moderate temperatures, coupled with spectacular scenic beauty, numerous lakes and recreation areas, state parks, sporting opportunities, exceptional fall color, and even occasional snow draw visitors to the region in all seasons. Everyone isn't an outdoor enthusiast, but those who aren't will enjoy exploring quaint towns and poking through antiques shops or searching for locally made arts and crafts. The region stretches from the state's northern border to the northeastern outskirts of Atlanta and includes the state's only ski resort, a Bavarian village, the birthplace of the Cabbage Patch Kids, and more down-home country cookin' restaurants than you can count.

SKY VALLEY

When it's cold enough to make snow, your family can schuss down the slopes at Georgia's only ski destination—**Sky Valley Resort** at the extreme northeast corner of the state near Dillard. Although the snow skiing season is limited, families can choose between a championship golf course, tennis, hiking, swimming, après-ski activities in season, and fine dining at the year-round resort. A wide variety of accommodations includes ski-in/ski-out

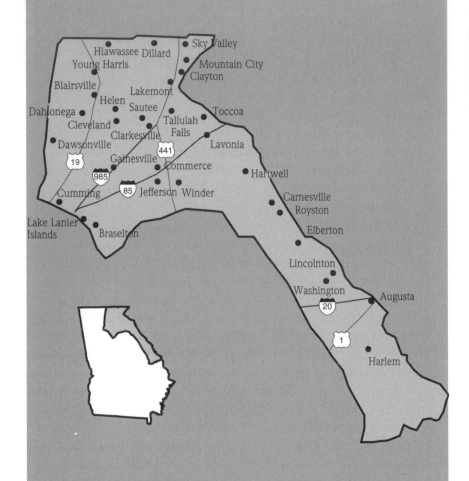

Northeast Georgia

chalets right on the slopes as well as rental homes—some of which offer fireplaces and Jacuzzis. To learn more about Sky Valley Resort, call (800) 437-2416. For information about accommodations, call (800) 262-8259.

DILLARD

A perennial favorite Dillard destination is the **Dillard House** on US 441. A year-round mountain resort perfect for families, it boasts a 100-year-old working farm, a petting zoo, tennis, swimming, horseback riding, a waterfall ride, and a Jacuzzi. Despite all these diversions, the most popular attraction here is the fabulous home cooking served family-style at the restaurant, which is open daily from 6:30 to 10:00 A.M. for breakfast, from 11:30 A.M. to 5:00 P.M. for lunch, and from 5:30 to 8:30 P.M. for dinner. Accommodations are offered in comfortable rooms, elegant suites, or cozy cottages. To find out more about the restaurant or the resort, call (800) 541-0671.

Dillard also offers fun for the whole family at **Andy's Trout Farm** on Betty's Creek Road. You can fish here for rainbow trout. No license is required; pole rentals and bait are available. Other facilities that attract families include cottages, a group camp, and hiking trails. The trout farm is open Monday through Saturday from 9:00 A.M. to 6:30 P.M. and Sunday from noon to 6:30 P.M. For more information, call (706) 746-2550.

The town of Dillard on US 441 is filled with antiques stores and shops filled with local mountain crafts. To find out more, call the Rabun County Convention and Visitors Bureau (706) 782-4812.

MOUNTAIN CITY

Just as it is today, at the turn of the twentieth century Mountain City was a popular mountain escape. The difference then was that the town boasted several rambling hotels and a large square-dancing hall. The dance hall is long gone, as are all the hotels with the exception of **The York House Bed & Breakfast** on York House Road. Built in 1896, the old hotel operates today as a B&B with country flair. Kids are welcome and enjoy the freedom of the extensive grounds with two streams, trails, a picnic area, and yard games. For more information or reservations, call (800) 231-YORK.

If your family loves camping and having fun in the outdoors, then a trip to **Black Rock Mountain State Park**, off US 441 north of Clayton, is sure to please. The park, the highest state park in Georgia, was named for the sheer black granite face of Black Rock Mountain. Active families participate in such open-air activities as picnicking, fishing, and hiking to scenic overlooks. Among the exhibits at the visitors center are animals, maps, and Foxfire memorabilia. If you'd like to stay overnight, you'll find cottages and camping. The park is open from 7:00 A.M. to 10:00 P.M. daily. For more information, call (706) 746–2141.

You may have read the series of *Foxfire* books or have seen the play and/or movie of the same name. What you may not have realized is that the books were about people in the North Georgia mountains and were prepared by students at Rabun County High School. Your children can explore the types of homes in which many of the mountaineers lived by visiting the **Foxfire Museum** (US 441), where artifacts from the series are displayed. The complex is open Monday through Friday from 10:00 A.M. to 4:00 P.M. To learn more about the museum, call (706) 746–5828.

CLAYTON

Clayton is a mecca for outdoor enthusiasts who flock to the area for almost every type of sport. If hiking appeals to your family, the Southeast is criss-crossed with trails blazed by Quaker naturalist William Bartram more than 200 years ago. Approximately 40 well-marked miles of the **Bartram Trail** wind through northeast Georgia. You can get trail maps and more infor-mation at the **Rabun County Welcome Center**, US 441, as well as details about horseback riding, snow skiing, water sports, and white-water rafting. The welcome center is open Monday through Friday from 9:00 A.M. to 5:00 P.M. Hours vary on the weekend, so it's best to call first. Call (706) 782–5113 to learn more.

Families with older children can experience the heart-pounding excitement of Class II to V white-water rapids on the **Chattooga Wild and Scenic River**, US 76, in the **Chattahoochee National Forest**. During the spring through fall season, several outfitters offer guided half-day, full day, and overnight raft trips on Section III and over the thirty rapids on Section IV. Among these outfitters are the **Nantahala Outdoor Center**, Chattooga

Ridge Road (800–232–7238), **Southeastern Expeditions,** US 76 (800–868–RAFT), and **Wildwater, Ltd.**, US 76 (800–451–9972). Because of the dangerous nature of this activity, age restrictions apply, so be sure to check ahead to make sure that none of your children is disappointed.

The area is laced with wildlife management tracts, recreation areas, and scenic regions—most of them in the **Chattahoochee National Forest.** Although the terrain is extremely rugged, families will find hunting, fishing, hiking, and primitive camping on the **Coleman River Wildlife Management Area**, Coleman River Road, part of the **Southern Nantahala Wilderness.** Energetic family members can hike past large old-growth timber alongside a stream tumbling through high boulders at the **Coleman River Scenic Area** on Forest Service Road 70. To learn more about outdoor activities available in these areas, call the Georgia Department of Natural Resources in Atlanta at (404) 535–5700.

Northeast Georgia's crystal-clear mountain lakes afford numerous family-oriented opportunities for boating, camping, fishing, hiking, and picnicking surrounded by spectacular mountain scenery. **Lake Burton**, on US 76 or State 197, offers 2,775 acres, 62 miles of shoreline, a public beach, and a marina. Smaller **Lake Rabun,** on Lake Rabun Road, has 835 acres and 25 miles of shoreline. Its **Rabun Beach Recreation Area** on County Road 10 features campsites with water and electrical hookups. For camping information, call (706) 782–3320. Primitive camping is available at tiny **Lake Seed**—240 acres and 13 miles of shoreline—located off Lake Rabun Road. Minuscule **Tallulah Falls Lake** on US 441 has 63 acres and 3% miles of shoreline. For more information on any of the lakes, call (706) 754–6036.

Children will love seeing the Georgia black bears, llamas, deer, peacocks, hawks, and eagles at **Tut Game Preserve** on US 441 and Seed Tick Road. Rated pilots participate in competitions and offer demonstrations at the facility's **Hang Glider Heaven.** Your family can stay in one of the preserve's five cabins and participate in its square dancing events. The preserve is open daily from 8:00 A.M. to 4:00 P.M. To learn more, call (706) 782–6218.

An ideal place for families to stay is the **English Manor Inn** on US 76E. In addition to the main inn, built in 1912, there are several smaller buildings with three to seven bedrooms and fully equipped kitchen facilities. Relax on one of the rocker-filled porches or in the swimming pool and Jacuzzi that lie beside a gurgling stream. A full country breakfast is served in the main inn. Special events occur throughout the year. For more information or reservations, call (800) 782–5780.

Home-style, wood-stove cooking served family-style attracts diners to the **Green Shutters Restaurant** on Main Street south of town. In pleasant weather you can dine on the screened-in porch overlooking the gardens and pastures filled with farm animals. The restaurant's gift shop carries Green Shutters specialty foods and cookbooks as well as other gift items. The restaurant is open daily except Tuesday from 8:00 to 10:00 A.M. for breakfast, from 11:00 A.M. to 2:00 P.M. for lunch, and from 5:00 to 9:00 P.M. for dinner. Call (800) 535–5971 for more information.

Incredible views of Warwoman Mountain combined with simply prepared, elegantly served, and reasonably priced meals bring dining families to the **Stockton House Restaurant** on Warwoman Road off US 23/441. The popular restaurant is open seven days a week year-round from 11:00 A.M. to 2:00 P.M. for lunch and from 5:00 to 9:00 P.M. for dinner. Reservations are not required but are recommended. To learn more, call (706) 782–6175.

LAKEMONT

The area surrounding Clayton is well known for its variety and quality of locally made arts and crafts. On weekends children like to watch woodworkers, weavers, and potters in their timber-framed studios at **Lofty Branch Arts and Crafts Village** on US 441S. In addition the village boasts a large, central gallery displaying the works of more than 200 regional and national artisans. The village is open daily from 10:00 A.M. to 5:00 P.M. To learn more, call (706) 782–3863.

If you want to get the feeling of what a mountain vacation in the 1920s might have been like, spend a night or two at the rustic **Lake Rabun Hotel** on Lake Rabun Road. Perched on a tree-shaded hillside overlooking the reservoir and primarily constructed of stone and wood, the hotel is furnished in primitive pieces handcrafted from rhododendron and twisted mountain laurel branches. The sixteen bedrooms are sparsely furnished; only one has a private bath. The common room, however, is well-stocked with games and magazines, and all the lake activities are only a stone's throw away. A delicious homemade breakfast is included in the room rate. For more information or reservations, call (706) 782–4946.

TALLULAH FALLS

Children are staggered by the view of **Tallulah Gorge** at US 441 and Old US 441. Reputed to be the oldest gorge in the United States, the 2-mile-long chasm is second in depth to the Grand Canyon at 1,100 feet deep. A system of trails and overlooks is available along the north rim of the canyon. Hiking into the ravine, however, is not recommended due to the rugged and treacherous terrain. Two parks offer access to the gorge. At the **Terrora Park and Visitors Center** see exciting exhibits about Tallulah Gorge and an interactive video on recreation and scenic opportunities in the northeast Georgia mountains. In addition, the park offers camping, picnicking, swimming, fishing, nature trails, and tennis. For more information on the park's campground, call (706) 754–6036; for information on the visitor center, call (706) 754–3276. At **Tallulah Gorge State Park**, US 441, you can camp, fish, hike, swim, or picnic. The park is open from 7:00 A.M. to 10:00 P.M. daily. To learn more, call (706) 754–8257.

TOCCOA

South on US 123 is the town of Toccoa, with specialty stores and fine restaurants in its downtown. For information on a historic walking tour, contact **Main Street Toccoa**, 203 North Alexander (706–886–8451). To acquaint the family with the history of the area, stop at the **Stephens County Historical Headquarters and Museum** at 313 South Pond Street. Located in a structure built in 1898, the museum displays artifacts from Indians, early settlers, and farmers of the area, as well as railroad memorabilia and mementoes once belonging to local famous persons. Call for an appointment. To learn more, call (706) 886–2132.

Henderson Falls Park, also in Downtown Toccoa, encompasses twenty-five acres of scenic attractions, including a beautiful waterfall, as well as play areas, an amphitheater, tennis courts, picnic pavilions, and a nature trail. For more information, call (706) 886–2132.

Currahee Mountain (Cherokee for "standing alone") on State 17 is an outlying peak of the Blue Ridge Mountains. If you're feeling adventurous you might want to hike to the 1,874-foot-high summit. To find out more about hiking as well as other outdoor activities here, call (706) 886–2132.

Enjoy a serene setting with a big surprise for the children on the campus of Toccoa Falls College on State 17 ALT. Stroll along a landscaped path to a placid pool, then look up to see the dramatic 186-foot **Toccoa Falls** plummeting from the cliff above. Nineteen feet higher than Niagara Falls, this cascade is a majestic sight. The path to the falls is open from 9:00 A.M. to sundown daily. To find out more, call (706) 886–6831.

Journey back to yesterday and see how early travelers fared by taking a guided tour of **Travelers Rest Historic Site** on Riverdale Road. The restored two-story plantation house was built in 1815 and expanded in 1833 to serve as a stagecoach inn. On the guided tour you can hear about famous guests, admire the simplicity of the original pieces with which the inn is furnished, and poke your head into the outbuildings. The inn is open for tours Tuesday through Saturday from 9:00 A.M. to 5:00 P.M. and Sunday from 2:30 to 5:30 P.M. For information, call (706) 886–2256.

Your family might enjoy a stay in the rustic lodge or in one of the eight cabins at **Trembly Bald Resort** on Yonah Dam Road. Authentic hand-hewn log cabins with kitchens, fireplaces, air conditioning, decks or porches, and anywhere from one to eight bedrooms will accommodate almost any size family. On a hot day you can cool off in the pool, creek, or lake. To find out more about the resort, call (706) 886–9069.

CARNESVILLE

Ask the children to imagine the clatter of horses' hooves as they passed over the board flooring of **Cromer's Mill Covered Bridge** on State 106. Only one span wide, the 132-foot-long viaduct over Nail's Creek was built in 1907 using the Town Lattice design. Present-day tourists will want to photograph the bridge to add to their collection of portraits of Georgia's covered bridges.

LAVONIA

Live bluegrass, country, and gospel family entertainment as well as special events are offered year-round at **Clem's Shoal Creek Music Park** at 3191 Providence Church Road. As an extra enticement, children younger than twelve are admitted free. For a schedule of events, call (706) 356–1092. There's never a shortage of activities for families at **Tugaloo State Park** off State 328. Situated on a rugged peninsula projecting into Lake Hartwell, the park offers tent and trailer sites, cottages, pioneer camping, a beach, boat ramps, docks, fishing, family/group shelters, waterskiing, hiking trails, miniature golf, and tennis. The park is open daily from 7:00 A.M. to 10:00 P.M. To find out more, call (706) 356–4362.

HARTWELL

Children may be amused by a naming tradition in Georgia. The state has the peculiarity of not giving towns names similar to or the same as the counties in which they are located. For example, Lumpkin is not in Lumpkin County and Clayton is not in Clayton County. A rarity in Georgia, therefore, is the town of Hartwell in Hart County. Both were named in honor of Nancy Hart, a Revolutionary War heroine. In fact, Hart County breaks with tradition in another way: It is the only county in Georgia named for a woman. Historic Hartwell features tree-lined streets of stately nineteenth-century homes, as well as specialty shops, clothing outlets, a variety of restaurants, and a historical society and museum. Special events during the year include a tour of historic homes, three community theater productions, April's Antique Boat Festival, and December's Home for the Holidays celebration. For more information about the town and county, call the chamber of commerce at (706) 376–8590.

Live family entertainment is presented every Saturday night at the **Bluegrass Music Express** (57 Depot Street), which features its own band—the Bluegrass Express—as well as guest bands, cloggers, and vocalists. Best of all, children are admitted free. For a schedule, call (706) 376–3315.

Native Americans not only met for their own councils but also to trade with white settlers at the Cherokee Indian Assembly Ground, which they considered to be the **Center of the World**. A roadside monument on US 29 honors the spot. Always accessible. No phone.

The family won't be satisfied with just one visit to **Hartwell Lake**.

Covering 56,000 acres and boasting 962 miles of shoreline, it is the largest artificial lake east of the Mississippi and one of the most popular recreation areas in the Southeast. Fed by two rivers that rise in the Blue Ridge Mountains, the water in the lake is purer than that of many municipal drinking water systems. Six miles wide, the lake has a depth of up to 200 feet and provides a home for more than twenty-one species of fish. The reservoir, part of which is in Georgia and part in South Carolina, offers camping, fishing, swimming, boating, picnicking, marinas, restaurants, an information center, and interpretive services. Public tours of the **Dam and Powerhouse** on US 29 on the Savannah River are available between June 1 and Labor Day. For more information about the lake, call (706) 376–4788. Lakefront cabins and campsites on Lake Hartwell are among the attractions at **Hart State Park** (330 Hart State Park Road), which is open from 7:00 A.M. to 10:00 P.M. daily. To find out more about the park, call (706) 376–8756.

If you want to look back at early county history, peruse the local historical artifacts displayed at the **Historical Society and Museum,** located in the 1800 one-story frame Victorian Teasley–Holland House at 31 East Howell Street. Have the youngsters find the picture of Nancy Hart and the replica of her musket among the antiques donated by local citizens. The museum is open from 8:00 A.M. to 5:00 P.M. Monday, Tuesday, Thursday, and Friday, as well as from 8:00 A.M. to 2:00 P.M. on Wednesday. To learn more, call (706) 376–8590.

ROYSTON

Baseball great Ty Cobb was from this small Georgia town. Fans of the game will want to see the **Ty Cobb Memorial**, a statue located outside City Hall on Franklin Springs Street. Memorabilia from the ballplayer's career are displayed at the library at 684 Franklin Springs Street and at the courthouse at 634 Franklin Springs Street. Both are open from 9:00 A.M. to 5:00 P.M. Monday through Friday. For more information about the Ty Cobb attractions, call (706) 245–7232.

Outdoor enthusiasts belong at **Victoria Bryant State Park** (1105 Bryant Park Road), surrounded by the rolling hills of the upper Piedmont region. One of only a few of Georgia's state parks that boasts a golf course, its challenging, well-manicured links offer nine holes. Anglers enjoy the stocked fish pond. The family can also enjoy swimming, hiking, camping, and picnicking here. The park is open from 7:00 A.M. to 10:00 P.M. daily. To find out more, call (706) 245–6270.

ELBERTON

Known as the Granite Capital of the World, Elberton is the center of a dynamic granite quarrying industry. The historic downtown, centered around Downtown Square, contains the 1893 granite-faced courthouse and jail, the 1910 depot, the **Granite Eagle Fountain**, other granite monuments, boutiques, galleries, and an old-fashioned soda fountain.

At the **Granite Museum** (1 Granite Plaza off State 72), the family can watch a film about how Elberton became the Granite Capital of the World. Then they can see the displays about granite products and examine antique stone-working tools. Other exhibits explain methods used for quarrying, sawing, polishing, cutting, and carving granite; still others relate the town's history. Don't leave without hearing the story of Dutchy, a statue of a Civil War soldier. Dutchy is the only statue we know of that actually had a funeral and burial but was later disinterred. The museum is open daily from 2:00 to 5:00 P.M. To learn more, call (706) 283–2551.

Children won't believe their eyes when they see the **Georgia Guidestones** sitting out in a field along State 77. Sometimes referred to as America's Stonehenge, the set of gargantuan granite monoliths contain a ten-part message for future generations transcribed in twelve languages. The stones are always accessible. There's no phone.

If fishing appeals to your family, then **Bobby Brown State Park** (2509 Bobby Brown State Park Road) is the place to go. It borders 78,000-acre **Clarks Hill Lake**—home of some of the best hybrid and striped bass fishing in the Southeast. The 665-acre park, located on the site where an eighteenth-century town thrived at the confluence of the Broad and Savannah rivers, features camping, a swimming pool, a boat ramp and dock, picnicking, waterskiing, and hiking. The park is open from 7:00 A.M. to 10:00 P.M. daily. To learn more about the park or the lake, call (706) 213–2046.

For a family outing not soon forgotten, try **Richard B. Russell Lake**. In addition to enjoying a variety of water sports, you can visit the

The Georgia Guidestones, located just outside of Elberton, add a little mystery to it all.

Powerhouse and Dam at 4144 Russell Dam Road. Two visitor centers are open Monday through Friday from 8:00 A.M. to 4:30 P.M. and weekends from 8:00 A.M. to 4:00 P.M. Guided tours of the powerhouse must be arranged two weeks in advance. To schedule a tour or for other information, call (706) 283–5121 or 283–8731. The beach at **Lake Richard B. Russell State Park** (2650 Russell State Park Road) is a popular place from which families can launch waterborne activities. It is, however, one of the state parks that does not offer camping. The park is open from 7:00 A.M. to 10:00 P.M. daily. For more information, call (706) 213–2045.

LINCOLNTON

Clarks Hill Lake borders nine counties and offers just about everything you need for family amusement: nine campgrounds, three county parks, five recreation areas, and four marinas. Formed by damming the Savannah River, the resultant lake with 1,200 miles of shoreline is the largest Corps of Engineers project east of the Mississippi. To find out more about the lake, call (706) 722–3770.

Children won't need to worry about having enough to do at **Elijah Clark State Park**, on Clarks Hill Lake off US 378. In addition to tent and trailer sites and cottages, the park offers a beach, boat ramps, picnic shelters, waterskiing, a hiking trail, and miniature golf. A museum displaying colonial artifacts from about 1780 is open weekends 9:00 A.M. to 5:00 P.M. The park itself is open daily from 7:00 A.M. to 10:00 P.M. Find out more about the park by calling (706) 359–3458.

The centerpiece of the **Lincoln County Historical Park** at 147 Lumber Street is the **May House,** former home of an early town doctor. Beautifully restored, the house is furnished with period pieces. The doctor's office is located in a separate building. The house and doctor's office are open only by appointment. To learn more, call the chamber of commerce at (706) 359–7970.

Your children can gain an appreciation of old-fashioned country stores at **Price's General Store** at 5021 Double Branches Road. One of the oldest still-operating rural general stores in Georgia, this is the place to go for groceries, bait and tackle, hardware, and hard-to-find items. The store is open from 6:30 A.M. to 6:00 P.M. Monday through Thursday, from 6:30 A.M. to 9:00 P.M. on Friday and Saturday, and from 8:00 A.M. to 6:00 P.M. on Sunday. To learn more, call (706) 359–4401.

AUGUSTA

Augusta is the state's second oldest city and the largest in the region. Founded in 1736, only three years after Savannah, Augusta began life as a remote trading post, but in 100 years developed into one of the busiest inland cotton markets in the world. The city served as the state capital from 1783 to 1795. Begin a visit to Augusta by stopping at the **Cotton Exchange Welcome Center and Museum** at 32 Eighth Street at Riverwalk. Constructed in 1886, the building was once the hub of Augusta's cotton market. Children are intrigued as they try to visualize the tremendous number of cotton bales that used to surround the structure. It was said that a child could hop from one bale to another for more than a mile without ever having to touch the ground. Today the building is filled with memorabilia describing the cotton industry from planting to manufacturing. In addition, the Cotton Exchange is the place to get information about activities, lodgings, and restaurants in Augusta. The welcome center is open Monday through Saturday from 9:00 A.M. to 5:00 P.M. and Sunday from 1:00 to 5:00 P.M. Call (706) 724–4067.

Outside the Cotton Exchange a brick courtyard leads to **Riverwalk**, a four-block, brick-paved esplanade atop a flood-prevention levee on the banks of the Savannah River. The heart of Augusta's tourist activity and site of many of the city's numerous festivals, the Riverwalk and immediately surrounding area feature gardens and landscaped slopes, an 1,800-seat amphitheater, restaurants, shops, an art museum, a 70-slip marina, and a children's playground. For more information, call (706) 821–1754.

For more than 100 years, the 9-mile **Augusta Canal** has provided not only a means of transporting goods but has also served as a source of many outdoor diversions. Canoeing and fishing are popular canal activities. In addition, the old towpath that runs alongside the canal provides opportunities for hiking, biking, picnicking, bird-watching, and environmental studies. Call the Augusta Canal Authority for more information at (706) 722–1071.

The clang–clang of the bell announces the arrival of the **Augusta Trolley**, an excellent way for the family to tour Augusta. Tours depart from the Cotton Exchange on Saturday mornings. Reservations are recommended. Call (706) 724–0436.

Your children will be interested in the artifacts from Augusta's past at the **Augusta–Richmond County Museum** at 560 Reynolds Street. The natural history exhibits go back to the formation of the earth and early human life on this planet. Among the kid-friendly attractions are an early filling station with cars pulled up to it, an 1877 fire engine, and a horse-drawn hearse. The museum is open Tuesday through Saturday from 10:00 A.M. to 5:00 P.M. and Sunday from 2:00 to 5:00 P.M. Call (706) 722–8454.

Horse lovers will be enthralled by the week-long **Augusta Cutting Horse Futurity and Festival**, the largest competition in the East and one of the top ten in the world. Totally western in flavor, the event is usually held in late January and features horse competitions, a cattle drive, and an exposition of cowboy wear and gear. To find out more about the Futurity, call (706) 724–0851.

Billed as the Water Sports Capital of the World, Augusta is the home of three annual world-class boating events that provide heart-pounding spectator excitement for families. The **Augusta International Rowing Regatta** is a 2,000-meter event that brings in Ivy League college athletes. In addition to the main event, a mini-festival features foot races and cycling contests. To find out more, call (706) 823–8374. The richest dragboat race in the world, the **Hardee's Augusta Southern National Drag Boat Race** features 100 hydroplane and flatbottom boats. Call (706) 724–2452 for more information. Competitors vie for the largest purse in American motorboat racing at **River Race Augusta**. For information on this, call (706) 860–6890.

Families may want to experience the river firsthand by taking a sightseeing voyage aboard the ***Princess Augusta,*** a replica of a paddle-wheel riverboat. For information about cruises including lunch, dinner, and moonlight voyages, call Augusta Riverboat Cruises at (706) 722–5020.

Your children will be interested in the stories connected with several Augusta monuments always accessible by car or on foot. The **Confederate Monument** (Seventh and Broad streets) honors the everyday Civil War soldier by placing a private on top and the generals around the base; the **Signer's Monument** (Greene and Gwinnett streets) lauds Georgia's signers of the Declaration of Independence; the **Haunted Pillar** (Fifth and Broad streets) is all that is left after a minister put a curse on the Marketplace; and a 176-foot chimney remains from the **Confederate Powder Works** (1717 Goodrich Street), an important manufacturer of gunpowder for the Confederacy.

The perpetual Christmas and Halloween displays at **Fat Man's Forest** at 1545 Laney Walker Boulevard provide a treat for the eyes. When we travel we often buy a Christmas ornament from each of the cities we visit. Fat Man's is a good store to start such a tradition for your family. Children are guaranteed to find a Halloween costume here, too. The shop is open from 10:00 A.M. to 6:00 P.M. Monday through Saturday with extended hours before holidays. Call (706) 722–0796.

Transport the family to a more uncomplicated time by spending the night at the **Partridge Inn** at 2110 Walton Way. Begun in 1879 as a private residence, the structure was expanded several times until it took its present form. One of the first all-suite inns in the country, the Partridge Inn is one of only three Georgia hostelries included in the National Trust for

Historic Preservation's prestigious Historic Hotels of America. A quarter-mile of verandas, a swimming pool, a formal dining room, and complimentary breakfast round out the amenities. To find out more or to make reservations, call (706) 737–8888.

The **Clarion Telfair Inn**, 326 Greene Street, isn't one hotel but seventeen turn-of-the-century houses occupying an entire block. Each house and every guest room is uniquely furnished and decorated. Facilities include a full-service restaurant, a lounge with live entertainment, a swimming pool with a hot tub, and tennis courts. For information or reservations, call (706) 724–3315.

If the family wants to lodge close to the river, Riverwalk, and the Cotton Exchange, an excellent choice is the **Radisson Riverfront Hotel Augusta** at Two Tenth Street. Although it is newly constructed, the design and brick exterior of the hotel blend well with the historic cotton warehouses surrounding it. A full-service hostelry, the Radisson provides a range of guest rooms and suites, a restaurant, a lounge, and a riverside swimming pool. Call (706) 722–8900 for more information or reservations.

HARLEM

Everyone of any age who has ever laughed at the antics of old-time movie comic Oliver Hardy will enjoy the activities at the **Oliver Hardy Festival** that is held the first Saturday of October in his birthplace. Family members young and old can enjoy the Laurel and Hardy movie marathon, professional Laurel and Hardy impersonators, Oliver Hardy look-alike contest, arts and crafts, good food, music, and more. To find out more about the festival, call (706) 556–3448.

WASHINGTON

Families can take a trip back in time at the working **Callaway Plantation** at Lexington Road/US 78W. Three homes here illustrate life in three periods of history in the area. First you can explore the red brick Greek Revival manor, which was built in 1869 and remains virtually unchanged. Each room is furnished in appropriate period pieces. Connected to the main house by a breezeway, the brick kitchen building is equipped much as it was when it was constructed. The two-story, four-room Federal Plain-style frame residence was built about 1800. It was the home of George R. Gilmer, who served as Georgia's governor for two separate terms in the 1820s and 1830s; it is furnished with pieces typical of the 1790s. Tykes are even more curious about the hewn log cabin. Built in about 1785, the hut probably served as a temporary residence while a more permanent one was under construction. The cabin features one room and a loft and contains primitive furniture and early domestic and agricultural tools. The plantation is open Tuesday through Saturday from 10:00 A.M. to 5:00 P.M. and Sunday from 2:00 to 5:00 P.M. Call (706) 678–7060 to find out more about the plantation and its special activities.

Children are fascinated by the Confederate gun collection and the Indian artifacts displayed at the **Washington Historical Museum** at 308 East Robert Toombs Avenue. Housed in a magnificently restored and furnished antebellum home, the collection can be seen Tuesday through Saturday from 10:00 A.M. to 5:00 P.M. and Sunday from 2:00 to 5:00 P.M. Call (706) 678–2105.

COMMERCE

Even the youngest among race fans can cheer on their favorite drivers at races run each weekend at the **New Atlanta Dragway** at 500 East Ridgeway Drive. Major events on the quarter-mile drag track include an annual bracket racing series. For more information or a schedule of events, call (706) 335–2301.

JEFFERSON

There's a grim fascination for youngsters in imagining what early methods of surgery must have been like. Few know that a Georgia doctor discovered the anesthesia that makes operations bearable. Exhibits at the **Crawford W. Long Museum** (28 College Street) describe Dr. Long and the development of anesthesia, as well as the history of Jackson County. Highlights include a typical 1840s doctor's office and a nineteenth-century general store. The museum is open Tuesday through Saturday from 10:00 A.M. to 5:00 P.M. and Sunday from 2:00 to 5:00 P.M. Call (706) 367–5307.

WINDER

An environmental, historical, and recreational opportunity for the whole family, **Fort Yargo State Park,** State 81S, is unique in that it caters to the disabled as well as everyone else. In addition to a lake, boating facilities, rental boats, fishing, a swimming pool, tennis courts, and a nature trail, the park features the Will-a-Way Recreation area, which provides handicapped-accessible cottages, food service, and a swimming beach. The park is open daily from 7:00 A.M. to 10:00 P.M. Call (770) 867–5313.

BRASELTON

Imagine a child's surprise when a replica of an eighteenth-century French chateau appears in a field alongside I–85. The castle-like structure houses the winemaking operations of the **Chateau Elan Winery and Resort**, 100 Tour de France. Everyone in the family can enjoy the tour and find out how wine is made; parents can partake in a tasting of the medal-winning wines. In addition, the chateau contains a museum, a gift shop in the form of a French street market, and two restaurants. Adjacent to the chateau is a luxurious inn and European health spa. Other amenities include nature trails, seasonal concerts, championship golf courses, a driving range, tennis courts, and an equestrian center. During the year the chateau comes alive with several special events. Among these are the July **Spirit of France Celebration,** which salutes Bastille Day; the August **Harvest Celebration,** where you can stomp grapes; and the **Lighting of the Chateau** on Thanksgiving Weekend, which kicks off the holiday season. Tours are conducted Monday through Friday from 11:00 A.M. to 4:00 P.M. and on weekends from 11:00 A.M. to 5:00 P.M. The gift shop is open from 10:00 A.M. to 9:00 P.M. daily. For more information about the winery, restaurants, inn, spa, or sporting facilities, call (800) 233–9463.

GAINESVILLE

Among the variety of attractions at **Brenau College** (#1 Centennial Circle) is the reconstructed **cabin of Cherokee Chief Whitepath.** The cabin is open Monday through Saturday from 10:00 A.M. to 5:00 P.M. and from 1:00 to 5:00 P.M. on Sunday year-round. Call (770) 535–8801. Also on campus is the **Bete Todd Wages Collection** of vintage clothing, which provides a time line of style changes. You can see the collection during normal business hours during the academic year. Call (770) 718–9830.

You can foster your children's interest in and appreciation of natural history at the **Elachee Nature Science Center** at 2125 Elachee Drive. In addition to the indoor museum exhibits, the 1,200-acre preserve offers botanical gardens and nature trails. Special family-oriented programs are offered throughout the year. The center is open from 10:00 A.M. to 5:00 P.M. Monday through Saturday, but the trails are open 8:00 A.M. to dusk daily. To find out more, call (770) 535–1976.

A variety of exhibits awaits your family at the **Green Street Station and Georgia Mountains Museum** at 311 Green Street, SE. Children are always absorbed by model train exhibits. This museum offers a particularly outstanding display, as well as a notable collection of railroad memorabilia. The museum boasts an exhibit honoring resident Ed Dodd and his comic strip *Mark Trail*, the first ecologically correct cartoon. History buffs are engaged by the papers of Civil War hero General James Longstreet. The museum is open Tuesday through Saturday from 10:00 A.M. to 5:00 P.M. Call (770) 536–0889.

Racing fans of all ages enjoy trips to Gainesville's tracks. At **Lanier Raceway's** three-eighth-mile oval track (State 53E) sanctioned NASCAR–Winston Racing Series events are run. For information, call (770) 967–2131. **Road Atlanta** (5300 Winder Highway) is the South's premier motorsports venue, where such luminaries as Paul Newman, Tom Cruise, and Walter Payton have tried their luck. For a schedule of events, call (770) 967–6143.

Known as the Poultry Capital of the World, Gainesville acknowledges this distinction through statuary found in the garden of **Poultry Park** at Broad and Grove streets. Another fun diversion for young children is the exquisitely crafted imported **Venetian Carousel** at the Lakeshore Mall (1285 West Washington Street). The carousel is accessible from noon to 8:00 P.M. Monday through Saturday and from 1:00 to 6:00 P.M. on Sunday.

CLARKESVILLE

A fantastic family retreat, the **Glen-Ella Springs Inn** on Bear Gap Road is a historic hotel built in 1890. Located on eighteen acres situated down an unpaved road, the inn has combined modern conveniences with the country charm of yesteryear. Most of the sixteen fetching guest rooms and suites in the rustic inn open onto rocker-filled porches with tranquil views. Surrounded by informal gardens, untouched forest lands, and nature trails along Panther Creek, the hostelry features a lobby with a soaring stone fireplace, as well as a large swimming pool and a garden shop. Breakfast is included in the room rate. In addition, the hotel boasts a gourmet restaurant featuring southern cuisine; it is open to the public for dinner by reservation. For information or reservations, call (706) 754–7295 or (800) 552–3479 from out of state.

For more than seventy years **La Prade's,** State 197 on the scenic shores of Lake Burton, has been serving up vast quantities of Southern fried chicken accompanied by platters mounded with vegetables, cornbread, biscuits, and desserts. In addition, since Lake Burton is noted for fine fishing, La Prade's offers a full-service marina, rental boats, and primitive cabins perfect for a fishing getaway. The restaurant is open May through October daily except Tuesday and Wednesday. Breakfast is 8:00 to 9:00 A.M.; lunch seatings are at 12:30 and 1:30 P.M.; dinner seatings are at 7:00 and 8:00 P.M. It is open weekends only in April and November and is closed between December 1 and March 31. To find out more about the restaurant or the fisherman's resort, call (706) 947–3312.

Children won't know what to look at first at **Mark of the Potter** on State 197. The building itself is a rustic 65-year-old water-powered gristmill, known as Grandpa Watts' Mill, located next to a small waterfall on the beautiful Soque River where there are pet trout to be fed. Artisans here are busy making wheel-thrown pottery, which is for sale. The lead-free crockery is oven, microwave, and dishwasher safe. In addition, the shop offers the handmade crafts of forty local artists—wood, metal, and ceramic jewelry, weavings, and hand-blown glass. The mill and shop are open every day except Christmas. From April through December the hours are 10:00 A.M. to 6:00 P.M.; from January through March the hours are 10:00 A.M. to 5:00 P.M. For more information, call (706) 947–3440.

Moccasin Creek State Park on State 197 on the shores of Lake

Burton is a wonderful place to begin a high-country adventure. In addition to campgrounds, the park—noted for its outstanding trout fishing—offers a fishing pier, boat ramp, dock, hiking trails, and picnicking. A special fishing section is reserved for angling by children younger than twelve and by senior citizens. Boating and water skiing are permitted, but there are no swimming areas. The park is open daily from 7:00 A.M. to 10:00 P.M. To find out more, call (706) 947–3194.

You'll have to do some real hiking to gaze on beautiful **Panther Creek Falls** in the **Panther Creek Recreation Area—Chattahoochee National Forest** on Old US 441. It's a 3½-mile hike one way to see the 80-foot falls. For more information, call (706) 754–6221.

CLEVELAND

Probably every child in America, as well as many others from around the world, is familiar with the cute, cuddly **Cabbage Patch Kids**—those one-of-a-kind soft-sculpture dolls. However, even few Georgians realize that they are the brainchildren of Cleveland resident Xavier Roberts. The moment a child steps into **BabyLand General Hospital** (19 Underwood Street) he or she enters a magical world where the Kids are delivered from Mother Cabbages by Licensed Patch Doctors and Nurses and placed for adoption. Children can let their imaginations run free when they hear "There's a cabbage in labor." Each Kid lives for the moment when some child adopts him into a loving home. Located in a turn-of-the-century medical clinic, BabyLand also offers clothing and accessories for the Kids, as well as Furskins Bears. Admission is free and visiting hours are Monday through Saturday from 9:00 A.M. to 5:00 P.M. and Sunday from 10:00 A.M. to 5:00 P.M. If you want to know more about BabyLand General, call (706) 865–5505.

Try your luck as a gold and gem prospector at the **Gold N' Gem Grubbin' Mine** on 75 Gold Nugget Lane. Between spring and fall you can also tour the operating mine. The complex also features a lake and a fishing stream. The mine is open daily from 9:00 A.M. to 6:00 P.M. Call (706) 865–5454.

Families desiring a completely secluded vacation place should check out **Villagio di Montagna** (US 129N) owned by Xavier Roberts of Cabbage Patch Kids fame. Nestled on sixteen wooded acres are picturesque Mediterranean-style, tile-roofed villas—many with Jacuzzi tubs and fireplaces. Palazzo rooms in the lodge overlook the river. Take a dip in the Olympic-size pool or pamper yourselves in the sauna and steam room. A complimentary breakfast is served each morning. To find out more or to make reservations, call (800) 367–3922.

SAUTEE

Introduce your children to a mound-building civilization of Native Americans as you point out the **Sautee-Nacoochee Indian Mound** at the intersection of State 75 and State 17. Built as long ago as 10,000 B.C., the mound later served as the burial place of two tragic lovers from warring Cherokee and Chickasaw tribes. In this century, a Greek-style temple was placed on top of the mound. Drive by anytime. There's no phone.

The **Old Sautee Store** at the intersection of State 17 and State 255 is a 100-year-old store/museum that lets you delve back into history. Although its old-timey items aren't for sale, its old store fixtures, antique posters, and merchandise from yesteryear convey a bygone way of life. Adjacent to the store is a sod-roofed cabin that serves as the Yule Log Christmas Shop. The museum is open year-round from 9:30 A.M. to 5:30 P.M. Monday through Saturday and from 1:00 to 6:00 P.M. on Sundays. Call (706) 878–2281.

You *can* buy the wares at the **Country Store at Skylake** (122 Sautee Trail). In addition to arts and crafts, the store carries picnic supplies and other sundries. More than a store, however, the emporium boasts an 1890s pharmacy stocked with ledgers, medicines, and other artifacts, as well as a model train chugging above an antique post office, and an old-fashioned marble-topped soda fountain where you can purchase hand-dipped ice cream, milk shakes, and other treats. From May through December the store is open from 9:30 A.M. to 5:00 P.M. Monday through Saturday and Sunday from noon to 5:00 P.M. It is closed from January through April. Call (706) 878–2292.

Don't leave the Sautee valley without stopping to photograph the **Stovall Covered Bridge** on State 255. Georgia's smallest covered bridge, it is only 33 feet long and one span wide. Built in 1895, it uses the Kingpost design. The road has been rerouted around the bridge, so if you blink you might miss it.

HELEN

Children crow with delight when the family pulls into the alpine village of Helen. They'll think they've been carried off to a German or Swiss Bavarian village and they won't want to return. Chalets, cobblestone alleyways, and shopkeepers dressed in lederhosen and dirndls create the old-world charm of the tiny hamlet. Bavarian favorites such as schnitzel, rouladen, and strudel are served in the many restaurants. More than 200 specialty and import shops sell Swiss and German merchandise. The newest additions to the shopping scene are factory outlet stores selling everything imaginable. Those who don't want to shop can find plenty of other activities here. Street entertainers may include jugglers, musicians, and face painters. You may find yourself recruited to participate in an impromptu Maypole dance. The calendar is loaded each year with more than thirty-five special events. Among the twenty-two motels, twenty-five cabin rentals, fifteen bed-and-breakfast inns, five condo/resorts, and eleven campgrounds, the area provides more than 1,000 accommodations. For more information about the town and its special events, call the Helen Welcome Center at (800) 858–8027 or the chamber of commerce at (800) 392–8279.

Family adventure awaits under the Big Wheel at **Alpine Amusement Park** on State 75. It offers exciting rides not only on a 40-foot Ferris wheel but on go-karts, bumper boats, and a tilt-a-whirl, as well as five kiddie rides. If that's not enough, the park features miniature golf and arcade games. During the summer months, the park is open daily from noon to 11:00 P.M.; the remainder of the year it is open on weekends only from noon to 10:00 P.M. Call (706) 878–2306.

A hike to **Anna Ruby Falls** (off State 356), a double waterfall high on the slopes of Tray Mountain, makes exercising a pleasure. Two creeks, the Curtis and the York, flow parallel to each other, dropping as side-by-side cascades. Curtis Falls plummets 150 feet, while York Falls plunges only 50 feet. A short, paved path leads from the visitor center to the overlook. Designed for the visually and mobility impaired is the Lion's Eye Nature Trail. The park is open from 10:00 A.M. to 8:00 P.M. daily. For more information, call (706) 878–3574.

It's all downhill on the 1-mile hike to the base of **Dukes Creek Falls** (State 348), which plummets 300 feet into a scenic gorge from the cliff above. At the bottom, kids enjoy wading in the stream or scrambling over the boulders in and alongside the brook. Some of the rocks make an excellent place to spread out a picnic lunch. After a memorable afternoon, the only problem is that it's all uphill to return to your car. For more information, call (706) 754–6221.

For the adventurous, horseback riding in the deep woods around Helen is an extremely popular family activity. You can choose from among these stables: **Culpeppers** (706–865–9802); **Chattahoochee** (706–878–7000); **Mountain Adventures** (706–865–5260); **Shamrock** (706–878–1608); and **Sunburst** (706–947–7433).

Children are charmed by the Bavarian chalet appearance of the main lodge at **Innsbruck Resort and Golf Club**, 11 Bahn Innsbruck, a resort just outside Helen. An ideal place for families, Innsbruck is an all-suite facility on 230 acres. Accommodations range from one-room suites to spacious four-bedroom homes. Most units feature a fireplace and offer a whirlpool tub, refrigerator, microwave, coffee maker, and a washer and dryer. In addition to sporting a unique eighteen-hole championship alpine golf course, the resort features tennis courts, two swimming pools, a hot tub, and a bar and grill. For information or reservations, call (800) 204–3536.

Pretend the family has been transported back to Helen's early days by visiting the **Museum of the Hills** in the Castle Inn building on State 75 downtown. An animated figure named Barney O'Feller conducts the old town tour and relates its history. A fun-filled finale at the museum is the Fantasy Village with Storyland buildings and fantasy characters. From April through November 15, the museum is open daily from 10:00 A.M. to 9:00 P.M.; the remainder of the year it is open from 10:00 A.M. to 6:00 P.M. To learn more about the museum, call (706) 878–3140.

Just as in the days of yore, grains are ground into meal at the **Nora Mill Granary** on State 75. Established in 1876, the mill used water power harnessed from the Chattahoochee River to propel the stone that ground the grain. Children can watch the same stone being used today to grind numerous grains, grits, and cornmeal. You can even request a custom mix. Open daily from 9:00 A.M. to 5:00 P.M., the mill sells its own special mixes, cookbooks, and homemade pies. For more information or mail orders, call (706) 878–2927.

Contributing to Helen's lighthearted atmosphere are numerous annual celebrations. The foremost festival is **Oktoberfest**, which actually lasts throughout September and October with live German bands, food and beverages, sing-alongs, and polkas and waltzes. Children enjoy the sights and sounds of **Alpenlights,** a winter lights festival that runs from mid-November to early February. Thousands of twinkling bulbs illuminate the old-world towers and gables as well as giant nutcrackers, candy canes, and fairy-tale characters. Before Christmas, business hours are extended and there are special trolley and carriage tours, storytelling, arts and crafts shows, a Dutch St. Nicholas celebration, and Glockenspiel characters that perform on the stroke of the hour. Special activities for children include a Christmas Market, a musical production, free Christmas ornaments, and dinner with Santa. The **Fasching Karnival** is a special Mardi Gras celebration in February or March. To find out more about these and Helen's other festivals, call (706) 878–2181.

With rustic log cabins ranging from one to six bedrooms, **Tanglewood Resort Cabins** on State 356 can accommodate almost any size family. Tucked away in seventy-five wooded acres adjacent to the Chattahoochee National Forest, each cabin is ensured of its privacy. Each features a fully equipped kitchen, fireplace, deck, grill, and picnic table. For more information or reservations, call (706) 878–3286.

A surefire, family-pleasing way to see Helen is aboard **The Toot Trolley**, which you can catch in front of Whitehorse Square. As you proceed slowly around the village, the driver regales you with tales of Helen's past. The authentic trolley runs Sunday, Monday, and Thursday from 11:00 A.M. to 6:00 P.M. and Friday and Saturday from 10:00 A.M. to 9:00 P.M. It does not operate on Tuesday and Wednesday. Children younger than eight ride free. For information, call (706) 219–2000. Another popular sightseeing tour is given in beautiful horse-drawn carriages. Contact **Horne's Buggy Rides** (706) 878–3658 or **Helen Carriage Works** (706) 878–3445.

If your family loves the outdoors, but finds roughing it a little too demanding, try **Unicoi State Park** on State 356, where you can stay in the comfort of the 100-room lodge with a restaurant or in rental cottages while enjoying the 1,081 acres of forest land, the lake, canoes, pedal boats, beach, hiking trails, fishing streams, lighted tennis courts, children's playgrounds, and picnicking areas. The park is open daily from 7:00 A.M. to 10:00 P.M. Call (706) 878–2201.

HIAWASSEE

From the minute your family arrives at the **Field Stone Inn** (on US 76 on the shores of Lake Chatuge), they'll have to make decisions about the enjoyable options available here. The marina has a boat ramp and free docking for guests. It also rents pontoon boats, fishing boats, and aquacycles, making all water sports easily accessible. The resort features an outdoor pool, an exercise room with a Jacuzzi, and lighted tennis courts. For the less energetic, who may want to take a leisurely stroll, read a book, or just look at the lake, the inn features paths, swings, and gazebos dotted around the property. For more information, call (800) 545–3408.

You can hardly top a country fair for memory-making family fun. Children are enthralled by demonstrations of pioneer skills such as blacksmithing, log splitting, and moonshine stilling, as well as by illustrations of such mountain crafts as woodcarving, pottery making, candle making, and quilting at the nearly month-long **Georgia Mountain Fair** in Hiawasee on US 76. Held each August, the fair also features food booths, clogging, and entertainment by Nashville headliners. Children younger than ten are admitted free. The fair is open Monday through Thursday from 10:00 A.M. to 9:00 P.M., Friday and Saturday from 10:00 A.M. to 10:00 P.M., and Sunday from 10:00 A.M. to 6:00 P.M. To check on the exact dates or for other information, call (706) 896–4191.

YOUNG HARRIS

Although there are oodles of activities within close driving range of the **Brasstown Valley Crowne Plaza Resort** on US 76, families may not even want to leave the property once they get there. Cradled in a 503-acre forest preserved as a bird sanctuary, the hotel is built on the site of a Cherokee Indian village dating back 10,000 years. A serene retreat, the resort is proclaimed as a prototype of an "environmentally correct" resort, with the ecological and cultural integrity of the land carefully preserved.

Accommodations are offered in a rustic inn or comfortable cottages. Although the contemporary hotel boasts modern amenities, the nostalgic hexagonal lobby is reminiscent of the national park lodges built at the turn of the century. Anchored by a 72-foot-tall fieldstone fireplace, the room features a vaulted ceiling, massive exposed beams, animals carved into the wooden posts, and antler chandeliers. Furnished in a mixture of Country English, Victorian, southern, and Appalachian mountains decor, most of the guest rooms in the main lodge enjoy breathtaking panoramas of Three Sisters Mountain or Brasstown Bald. Each of the eight secluded four-bedroom cottages features a fully equipped kitchen and a family room with a fireplace and reflects a different mountaineering motif. Brasstown Valley Resort boasts two restaurants, a lobby lounge, a 7,100-yard championship Scottish links–style golf course, a tennis center with lighted courts, a health spa with exercise equipment, an indoor/outdoor pool, interpretive hiking trails, and trout fishing. To discover the natural wonders of Brasstown Valley, call (800) 201–3205.

Though always abounding in a tremendous number of activities for children, Brasstown Valley provides special attention to kids during the **Brasstown Valley Family Summer Adventure Package**. Organized children's adventures at the Brasstown Valley **Mountaineers Kids Club** include craft making using natural mountain treasures, ancient artifact observations, storytelling, wildlife hikes, and pool Olympics. The package includes accommodations for four, the breakfast buffet daily, two hours of tennis daily, use of the health and fitness center, and two for one admission to the Kids Club. For more information, call (800) 201–3205.

Music, stories, and tall tales relating to the mountaineers of north Georgia will charm all the members of the family at **"The Reach of Song"** **Appalachian Drama** performed on the campus of Young Harris College on US 76. Running Tuesday through Saturday nights from the end of June through the end of August, the story focuses on how the main character, local resident Byron Herbert Reece, found the inspiration and support to become a writer. In addition to the performances, other activities attract young and old alike: arts and crafts are displayed for sale; ole-timey music accompanies a dinner on the grounds each evening; and a special arts festival is held early in the season. All seats are reserved and there is limited seating, so it's best to purchase tickets ahead of time to avoid disappointment. For more information, call (800) 262–7664.

BLAIRSVILLE

You'll all marvel at the view of four states from the summit of **Brasstown Bald Mountain** off the State 180 Spur near Blairsville. At 4,784 feet in elevation, the peak is the highest spot in Georgia. Drive most of the way up the mountain to the parking area and stop in at the log cabin bookstore where you can buy postcards, books about the area, souvenirs, and locally made arts and crafts. It's only a half-mile from there to the peak but the way is steep. You have two options: you can walk up the paved path that has several benches and rest areas along the way or you can purchase a ride on the shuttle. Either way, once you reach the top, enjoy the view and stop in at the Visitor Information Center where you can see a film and examine several exhibits. Four trails of varying degrees of difficulty ranging from one-half to 6 miles in length branch off from the parking area. Brasstown Bald is open daily from 10:00 A.M. to 6:00 P.M. from Memorial Day through October as well as spring and fall weekends depending on the weather. For more information, call (706) 896–2556.

The twisting **Russell-Brasstown Scenic Byway** (State 17/75 to State 180 to State 348 to State 75 ALT) is a 38-mile loop guaranteed to offer breathtaking views of the scenic mountains and valleys. Several scenic overlooks and interpretive signs are placed along the route.

Families can horse around at **Trackrock Stables** at 4890 Trackrock Campground Road. For the casual rider, there's a one-hour ride through mountain meadows and tree-shaded paths alongside gushing streams. More adventurous riders can canter over fields and hillsides and gallop through the meadows. Real horseback riding diehards can spend the night, a week, or longer at the campground or in a rental cabin. Nonriders in your family can go on a hayride or spend their time fishing or swimming. Children of all ages are welcome. The stable is open year-round, but it's best to make a reservation before you arrive. For more information, call (706) 745–5252.

A great place for an inexpensive family outing, the area around Blairsville is peppered with diversions for outdoor enthusiasts: national forest, waterfalls, lakes, and recreational areas. **Helton Creek Falls** (off US 19/129) is actually three falls hidden in a deep hardwood forest. **Lakes Nottley** (US 19/129) and **Winfield Scott** (State 180) provide boat docks, camping, fishing, swimming, and picnicking. For information on Lake Nottley, call (706) 745–5789; for more about Lake Winfield Scott, call (706) 754–6221. Recreation areas, including **Cooper's Creek Scenic Area** (Forest Service Road #4; 706–632–3031); **High Shoals** (Forest Service Road #283; 706–745–6928); **Sosebee Cove** (State 180; 706–745 6928); and **Woody Gap** (State 60; 706–864–6173), provide hiking trails, fishing, camping, and picnicking.

Located within the Chattahoochee National Forest, **Vogel State Park** (off US 19/129) is a haven for families. The 280-acre park features campsites, cottages, a lake with swimming and pedal boats, miniature golf, playgrounds, and picnicking. A favorite of both casual and serious hikers, the park provides 17 miles of trails including an access connection to the Appalachian Trail. The park is open daily from 7:00 A.M. to 10:00 P.M. To learn more about Vogel State Park, call (706) 745–2628.

Winding roads can lead to adventure, and twisting, turning US 19/129 between Dahlonega and Blairsville leads to the **Walasi-Yi Center**, the only covered point on the 2,000 mile Appalachian Trail. The stone shelter, built at Neel's Gap in the 1930s by the CCC, stocks necessities such as groceries and hiking gear, as well as mountain crafts and regional books and maps. The facility is open Monday through Friday from 9:00 A.M. to 5:00 P.M. and weekends from 8:00 A.M. to 6:00 P.M. For more information, call (706) 745–6095.

DAHLONEGA

The entire family will get gold fever with a visit to this small town. Family members may not realize that the first major gold rush in America was in Dahlonega in 1828. In fact, the word *Dahlonega* is from the Cherokee name for "precious yellow metal." The easily recognized phrase "Thar's gold in them thar hills" originated during that gold rush. Although the area was virtually abandoned by prospectors when a richer gold seam was discovered in California, millions of dollars worth of the gold ore have been extracted from the mountains—often using primitive methods. It is

The whole family will enjoy relaxing and cooling off at Helton Creek Falls near Blairsville.

believed, however, that enough gold still remains to pave the square around the courthouse 1 foot deep in the precious metal. At one time Dahlonega was home to a branch of the U.S. Mint; it produced more than $6 million in gold coins in just twenty-three years. Not only is the tower at North Georgia College gilded with the yellow ore, but the state's Capitol dome in Atlanta is covered in gold from the north Georgia mountains. To learn more about Dahlonega, call the chamber of commerce at (800) 231–5543.

Visiting the **Dahlonega Courthouse Gold Museum,** Public Square, is an excellent way for your children to learn more about gold mining. Housed in the old courthouse, the museum is the second most visited historic site in the state. A film and exhibits tell the story of the gold rush and describe mining techniques as well as lifestyles of old-time prospectors. A child's mouth will drop open in awe when he or she gets a look at the large gold ingot (highly secured, of course). The museum is open from 9:00 A.M. to 5:00 P.M. Monday through Saturday and from 10:00 A.M. to 5:00 P.M. on Sunday. For more information, call (706) 864–2257.

Thrills and chills on the Chestatee and Etowah rivers are guaranteed whether you take a half-hour or overnight guided canoe, kayak, or tube trip with **Appalachian Outfitters** on State 60S. The company also offers canoe clinics and equipment rentals. The outfitters operate from March through October. Reservations are strongly suggested. To learn more, call (706) 864–7117.

For even more family fun, a visit to **Blackburn Park** on Auraria Road is sure to please everyone. The home of the **Dahlonega Bluegrass Festival,** held in June, the park also provides an archery range, gold panning, camping, swimming, fishing, and hiking. Call (706) 864–3711 for more information.

A fascinating place for anyone interested in learning about wine production is **Cavender Castle Winery** on Wimpy Mill Road. Georgia's only bed-and-breakfast/winery, the mountain-top edifice was constructed to resemble a castle with old-world ambience. After touring the operation, parents can enjoy tasting several of the award-winners. A gift shop sells wine-related items. Picnic tables in the shadow of the castle provide an excellent place to savor an informal meal while enjoying the sweeping mountain views. From spring through fall the Cavender Castle is open daily except Wednesday; the remainder of the year it is open only Friday through Sunday. For more information, call (706) 864–4759.

Help your youngsters get an idea of what gold mining was like by taking them to **Consolidated Mines** at 125 Consolidated Road. Although the excavation closed in 1900, it was once the largest operating mine east of the Mississippi. Tours explore 250 feet into the tunnel systems. Children can also experience the excitement of gold panning or purchasing a trinket from the souvenir shop. The mine is open from 10:00 A.M. to 4:00 P.M. daily. Call (706) 864–8473.

Children may strike it rich panning for gold and gemstones at **Crisson Gold Mine** (US19/Wimpy Mill Road), which began operation in 1847. Reopened in 1970 as a gold panning destination, the mine is run by the fourth generation of a gold mining family. Just so that no one will miss an opportunity to make his or her fortune, indoor panning is offered during the winter season. You can purchase gold, gold nuggets, and gold jewelry in the gift shop. Crisson's is open daily year-round. On weekends and during the entire summer Crisson's is open from 10:00 A.M. to 6:00 P.M.; the rest of the year it is open from 10:00 A.M. to 5:00 P.M. Call (706) 864–6363 or 864–7998.

If your family loves camping and having fun in the outdoors, you'll want to visit the **DeSoto Falls Scenic Area—Chattahoochee National Forest** on US 19/129N. Because the elevation varies between 2,000 and 3,400 feet in a very small area, the streams that flow through the area plunge from the higher level to the lower level in three separate waterfalls. Two are reached by easy hiking trails; the third requires a strenuous hike to see. Among the other activities at the park are fishing and picnicking. The park is open daily from 7:00 A.M. to 10:00 P.M. For more information and a recreation guide, call (706) 864–6173.

A good place to introduce the children to astronomy is the **George E. Coleman, Sr. Planetarium** on the campus of North Georgia College. When the college is in session, regularly scheduled shows are given on Friday evenings at 8:00 P.M. Special shows are given by appointment. To find out more, call (706) 864–1511.

Medicine Bow on Wahsega Road offers a very special set of activities sure to capture the imagination of each family member. Essentially an outdoor school imparting the skills of the Native Americans who first resided in the area, Medicine Bow offers such programs as the Weekend of the Bow, which includes instruction, archery adventures, games, and contests; Parent/Child Adventures, which explore the skills and games of Native Americans; Nature by Canoe, which provides not only instruction in canoeing skills but a naturalist's view of the river; Weekends with the Earth, which offers spring and fall botanical studies of plants and their uses as food, medicine, and crafts; Stalking and Tracking, which teaches the gaits, prints, and track patterns of indigenous animals; and Spirit Path, which demonstrates ways to lead a life aligned with the earth. Summer camps are also run for children ten and older. To find out more about this unique operation, call (706) 864–5928.

For the truly venturesome, **Mountain Adventures Cyclery, Inc.** (State 400 and State 60 at Long Branch Station) rents mountain bikes and provides guided trail tours for all levels of experience. The shop is open on weekdays except Tuesday from 10:30 A.M. to 6:30 P.M. and on weekends from 9:30 A.M. to 5:00 P.M. To find out more, call (706) 864–8525.

For a meal beyond belief, take the entire family to the **Smith House** (202 South Chestatee Street), world renowned for its bounteous meals served family style. You'll probably have to wait in line for a meal of Southern fried chicken and honey-cured country ham accompanied by mountainous platters of vegetables and other side dishes. In addition, the Smith House offers B&B accommodations and sports a swimming pool. The restaurant is open on Sunday from 11:00 A.M. to 7:30 P.M.; Tuesday through Thursday from 11:00 A.M. to 3:00 P.M. for lunch and from 4:00 to 7:30 P.M. for dinner; and Friday and Saturday from 11:00 A.M. to 3:00 P.M. for lunch and 4:30 to 8:00 P.M. for dinner. In general, the restaurant is closed on Mondays, but call to check because it is open on Mondays during the fall leaf season and on Mondays of holiday weekends. Call (706) 864–3566 for more information.

Among the many family-oriented festivals that fill Dahlonega with fun-filled activities all year long are the **World Gold Panning Championship** in April, the **Wildflower Festival of the Arts** in May, the **Dahlonega Bluegrass Festival** in June, **Gold Rush Days** in October, and an **Old-Fashioned Christmas Celebration** in December. For information on any of these festivals, contact the chamber of commerce at (706) 864–3711.

DAWSONVILLE

Children will be awestruck when gazing at 729-foot **Amicalola Falls**, the highest waterfall east of the Rockies. Located in **Amicalola Falls State Park**, off State 52, the falls is one of the Seven Natural Wonders of Georgia. You can drive up to the foot of the falls or hike part of the way up from the bottom or part of the way down from the top. Nestled on top of the mountain is a fifty-seven-room lodge with an all-you-can-eat buffet restaurant serving breakfast, lunch, and dinner. In addition, the park offers cabins, camping facilities, hiking trails, picnicking, and interpretive programs. The park is open daily from 7:00 A.M. to 10:00 P.M. Call (706) 265–8888 to find out more.

A day's escape from the hustle and bustle of the modern world can be yours by spending the day with **Amicalola River Rafting Outpost** on State 53W. It offers rafting and tubing trips down the Amicalola River, as well as hiking and cabins with hot tubs. Call (706) 265–6892.

Hiking enthusiasts can access Georgia's 78 miles of the 2,000-mile **Appalachian Trail** from an 8-mile approach trail from Amicalola Falls State Park to Springer Mountain. Find out more about the trail by calling (706) 265–6278 or 265–8888.

In the autumn, children marvel at the orange sea of pumpkins at **Burt's Pumpkin Farm** on State 52N. Folks come from miles around to choose that perfect pumpkin for their Halloween jack-o'-lantern. An even more popular weekend activity, however, is the tractor-pulled hayride—a 2-mile trip past two of the pumpkin fields, over a covered bridge, and within sight of Amicalola Falls. If you've never seen popcorn being processed, you can watch the process at Burt's. Open only from September through October, the farm also sells gourds, squash, and Indian corn. The farm is open daily 9:00 A.M. to 5:00 P.M. during those two months. Call (706) 265–3701.

Back-to-nature types enjoy exploring the **Dawson Wildlife Management Area** on State 318W, which encompasses 18,000 acres of public hunting, fishing, canoeing, hiking trails, and primitive camping. Because of the hilly terrain, four-wheel-drive vehicles may be required in some areas. The area is open twenty-four hours a day except during hunting season, when the area is restricted to hunters. For more information, call (404) 535–5700.

When it's time for dinner, take the kids for great hamburgers and fries at the **Dawsonville Pool Room** on East First Street. It houses such disparate collections as memorabilia from local resident Bill Elliott's NASCAR career and relics from early moonshine runners. The pool room is open Sunday through Thursday from 7:00 to 10:00 P.M. and Friday and Saturday from 7:00 to 11:00 P.M. Call (706) 265–2792.

Auto racing fans in the family can enjoy the **Elliott Museum and Souvenir Center** (State 183), home of famed race driver Bill Elliott's operation. In addition to a video about Elliott's career, see memorabilia and race cars. A showroom and gift shop are open Monday through Saturday from 9:30 A.M. to 4:30 P.M. Call (706) 265–2718.

CUMMING

One of Atlanta's premier annual events is the **Atlanta Steeplechase** at Seven Branches Farm. A visit here makes a gala day in the country for families. Usually held in early April, the day consists of watching brightly bedecked jockeys put gorgeous thoroughbreds over brush jumps in six to seven races, as well as people watching and picnicking. Ticket sales are in advance only. For information or tickets, call (404) 237–7436.

Good foot-stomping, hand-clapping family fun can be had at **Lanierland Country Music Park** (6115 Jot'em Down Road), which presents top-name country music entertainment in two shows per night from May to November. Call (770) 887–7464 for information and a schedule of events.

Covered-bridge fans will want to search out **Pooles Mill Covered Bridge** on Pooles Mill Road. Take State 20 west of Cumming to Ducktown, then go 3 miles north to Heardsville, then go 1 mile north on Pooles Mill Road. Spanning Settendown Creek, the 90-foot-long, one-span-wide bridge was built in 1906.

LAKE LANIER ISLANDS

A family entertainment mecca, Lake Lanier Islands (6950 Holiday Road) is a full-service resort including 1,200 acres of recreational facilities surrounded by 38,000 acres of waterborne activities. Youngsters won't have to worry about having enough to do or having to wait in line for a turn at the **Lake Lanier Beach and Water Park,** which boasts ten water slides, an 850,000-gallon wave pool with nine types of waves, a half-mile beach, and an area for tiny tykes with a Kiddie Lagoon and Wiggle Waves. The water park is open from 10:00 A.M. to 6:00 P.M. on weekdays and from 10:00 A.M. to 7:00 P.M. on weekends from Memorial Day to Labor Day. It is also open on weekends in May and the weekends after Labor Day in September. To find out more about any of the facilities, call (770) 932–7275.

In October, kids can get into the action at Lake Lanier by entering the jack-o'-lantern carving contest at the **Great Pumpkin Arts & Crafts Festival.** Other family-oriented activities include Georgia's largest pumpkin competition, arts and crafts exhibits, country and bluegrass music, clogging, carnival rides, boat rides, and pony rides. For more information, call (770) 932–7200.

Everyone in the family will love the sights and sounds of the spectacular animated holiday light show, **Magical Nights of Lights**, which features a million lights sprinkled throughout the 1,200-acre resort from mid-November through New Year's Day. Scenes include Reindeer Forest, Santa's Castle, Frosty's Playland, Birds of Paradise, and many more. Children can roast marshmallows and visit with Santa. To find out more about the festival, call (770) 932–7200 if you live in the metro Atlanta area or (800) 840–LAKE from the rest of the state.

Sprawling over a wooded peninsula overlooking the lake, the **Lake Lanier Islands Hilton Resort** (7000 Holiday Road) is a perfect spot for a family getaway. With 224 rooms and three restaurants, the resort offers a wide selection of year-round activities. The eighteen-hole, par-72 championship golf course has been described by *Golf Digest* magazine as the "Pebble Beach of the Southeast." Other recreational activities include three lighted tennis courts, lighted jogging trails, a heated pool, a health club with weight equipment, three whirlpools, two steam saunas, boating, fishing, and a playground. To learn more about the resort, call (800) 768–LAKE.

Also overlooking the lake, the **Stouffer Renaissance PineIsle Resort** (9000 Holiday Road) is a four-star, four-diamond property ideal for families. The 250-room hotel offers several suites and twenty-eight spa rooms as well as regular guest rooms. Recreational options include fishing, an eighteen-hole championship golf course, a heated indoor/outdoor pool, a health club, a marina, and both outdoor and enclosed tennis courts. Children's activities are scheduled during the summer. Call (770) 945–8921.

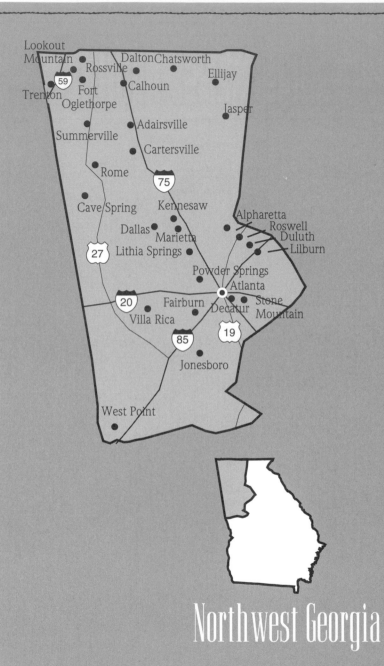

Northwest Georgia

NORTHWEST GEORGIA

Northwest Georgia has seen momentous historical events. At one time, the region served as the capital of the Cherokee Nation, largest of the Five Civilized Tribes of the Southeast. The Cherokee who farmed here lived in log homes and had both a written language and a constitution. During the Civil War the Confederacy won one of its most stunning victories in northwest Georgia and put up tremendous resistance to advancing Federal troops, although ultimately they were unable to keep the Union from taking Atlanta. In fact, so much Native American and Civil War history is associated with the northwestern corner of the state that two trails have been devised to link these attractions. The **Chieftains Trail** explores the remnants of three Native American civilizations that flourished here. For more information about the trail, call (706) 295–5576. The **Blue and Gray Trail** traces the events of Union General William Tecumseh Sherman's campaign from the northern border of the state to the Battle of Atlanta. To find out more about this trail, call (706) 629–3406.

In addition to human history, the region abounds with natural attractions. The **Chattahoochee National Forest** encompasses 864,359 acres in north Georgia and provides scenic rivers for fishing, canoeing, rafting, and kayaking; hiking trails such as the Appalachian, Benton MacKaye, and William Bartram Trails; horseback riding trails; six state parks; five major lakes, and the Cohutta Wilderness. The region is characterized by diminutive villages but also contains small cities such as Dalton, Calhoun, and

Rome. In the extreme southern part of the region, in the foothills of the Appalachian and Blue Ridge Mountains, is vibrant, sophisticated Atlanta—Capital of the New South. All in all, if your family chooses to explore this region, you'll find a wealth of intriguing historical places and scenic spots.

ROSSVILLE

John Ross was an important Cherokee Nation chief. Visiting the **John Ross House** on McFarland Avenue is a good way for children to learn more about Native American history. The two-story log cabin in which he lived was built in 1797 by his Scottish grandfather. The house is open daily from June through September from 1:00 to 5:00 P.M. To learn more about the house and the Chieftains Trail, call (706) 295–5576.

A family fun center, **Lake Winnepesaukah Amusement Park** (one mile off US 27) offers a carousel, paddle boats, a roller coaster, other rides, and picnic areas. Entertainment is offered on Sundays. From May through Labor Day the park is open Thursday through Sunday from noon to 11:00 P.M.; it is open weekends only in April and September. For information, call (706) 866–5681.

LOOKOUT MOUNTAIN

The Battle for Chattanooga in 1863 was one of the most important battles of the Civil War. Children and adults can understand the battle by visiting the **Battles for Chattanooga Museum** (3742 Tennessee Avenue), which includes a three-dimensional presentation of the battle containing 5,000 miniature soldiers, 650 lights, and sound effects. If you visit during the summer, your children will have the opportunity to learn about the everyday life of a foot soldier from reenactor Sergeant "Fox Jim" McKinney. The museum is open 8:30 A.M. to 8:30 P.M. between Memorial Day and Labor Day; 9:00 A.M. to 5:00 P.M. the remainder of the year. It is closed Christmas Day. For more information, call (706) 820–2531.

Just imagine the thrill of soaring like a bird. Although youngsters won't be trying the sport for several more years, they can watch hang gliders launch themselves from 1,340-foot McCarty's Bluff at **Lookout Mountain Flight Park and Training Center** on Lookout Mountain Parkway (State

189). If teens and parents are extra brave, they can take lessons from a certified instructor. The flight park is open daily year-round from 9:00 A.M. to 6:00 P.M. with the exception of being closed Wednesdays and Christmas Day. To find out more, call (706) 398–3541 or (800) 688–LMFP.

Children can find a tremendous number of attractions for them at legendary **Rock City Gardens** at 1400 Patten Road atop Lookout Mountain. Everyone will enjoy exploring the fourteen-acre natural rock garden with its lush landscaping, waterfalls, unusual rock formations, and a legendary view of seven states from Lover's Leap. Children are particularly delighted with the underground scenes found in Fairyland Caverns and the live fairy-tale characters who inhabit Mother Goose Village. Prospector's Point is a new gemstone sluice. Families can visit the numerous shops, including a Christmas Shop, and eat at one of several restaurants. Several special events are scheduled throughout the year, the most popular of which is **Rock City's Fairy Tale Festival**, held three weekends in August. Storytellers, puppeteers, clowns, magicians, and singers delight children of all ages. Rock City is open year-round every day (except Christmas) from 8:30 A.M. to sundown. To learn more about the park and special events, call (706) 820–2531.

Your family can stay within walking distance of Rock City Gardens at the **Chanticleer Inn** at 1300 Mockingbird Lane. Now a bed-and-breakfast, the charming stone cottages of the inn, some of which boast a fireplace, were built in the 1930s. Other amenities include a playground and an outdoor pool. A delicious complimentary breakfast is included in the price. To learn more or to make reservations, call (706) 820–2015.

FORT OGLETHORPE

Fort Oglethorpe was once the home of the Sixth Cavalry of the U.S. Army. Located on the parade field of the former fort is the **Sixth Cavalry Museum**, dedicated to showcasing the lives of mounted military men. Children can acquaint themselves with that bygone era by examining artifacts including clothing, equipment, pictures, historic documents, and other relics pertaining to the cavalry. The museum is open May through November, Monday through Friday from 10:00 A.M. to 4:00 P.M. and Saturday, 1:00 to 4:00 P.M. For more information, call (706) 861–2860.

One of the most important victories for the Confederacy was at

Chickamauga, Georgia, but that conflict was followed by a staggering loss at Chattanooga, Tennessee. The battlegrounds of both campaigns were combined into the **Chickamauga and Chattanooga National Military Park** on US 27. A fascinating place for those who are interested in Civil War history, it is the nation's oldest military park as well as the largest. Begin exploration of its 8,000 acres at the Chickamauga Visitor Center. A multimedia orientation presentation recounts the details of the battle and the origin of the National Military Park System. Children are awestruck by the Fuller Collection, a 355-weapon accumulation of military shoulder arms spanning the period from the Revolutionary War to World War II. The battlefield has an 8-mile driving tour, as well as walking, hiking, bicycling, and bridle trails. Numerous historical markers help all family members understand the progress of the bloody two-day battle; many monuments honor the men of both sides who fought here. You can almost hear the sounds of battle. One log cabin from the era survives, and another has been reconstructed. Both had served as officers' headquarters. The visitor center is open from 8:00 A.M. to 5:45 P.M. from Memorial Day to Labor Day and 8:00 A.M. to 4:45 P.M. the remainder of the year. The visitor center is, however, closed on Christmas Day. To find out more, call (706) 866–9241.

TRENTON

Discover a serene habitat overflowing with natural attractions at **Cloudland Canyon State Park** on State 136 in extreme northwest Georgia. Located on Lookout Mountain, the 2,000-acre park attracts families and others who appreciate rugged terrain. Paved and dirt hiking trails skirt both rims of the canyon, providing breathtaking views. You'll pass through millions of years of geological history as you hike down into the canyon, the only place from which you can see the park's spectacular waterfalls. Other family-oriented activities include fishing, tennis, picnicking, and swimming. Accommodations are offered in fully equipped cottages, or, if your family likes to camp, you may choose tent, trailer, or primitive camping sites. The park is open daily from 7:00 A.M. to 10:00 P.M. For more information, call (706) 657–4050.

DALTON

Dalton is known as the Carpet Capital of the World and offers 150 carpet mills and 100 carpet outlet stores. We were surprised to learn that bedspread tufting led to the carpet industry. Your family can find out more about how that came about at **Crown Gardens and Archives** (715 Chattanooga Avenue), a local history center located in a historic building constructed in 1884. The facility is open Tuesday through Friday from 10:00 A.M. to 5:00 P.M. and Sunday from 10:00 a.m to 3:00 P.M. To learn more, call (706) 278–0217.

If carpet history doesn't interest you, llama trekking in the Chattahoochee National Forest is almost guaranteed to attract your family's attention. At **Hawksbell Farm** (1618 Dawnville Road), you do the hiking but llamas carry your gear, including lunch and hammocks to use for an afternoon snooze before you start back. For information, call (706) 259–9310.

More than 150 years old, three-story **Prater's Mill** (848 Shugart Road) was used as a campsite by both Union and Confederate troops during the Civil War. Your family can enjoy the grounds and have a picnic there anytime, but the mill is only open and operational for a weekend in both May and October during the **Prater's Mill Country Fair,** when more than 200 artists and craftspeople set up their wares. The fairs include wonderful food, musical entertainment, and other activities. To find out more, call (706) 275–6455.

CHATSWORTH

Carter's Dam, at the junction of US 411 and State 136, impounds the Coosawattee River into 3,220-acre **Carter's Lake,** a mecca for water sports enthusiasts. Reputed to be the deepest lake east of the Mississippi, the reservoir boasts eight public-use areas sure to please any family. For more information about the lake, call (706) 334–2248. **Carter's Lake Marina and Resort** (Resource Office Road) offers a variety of amenities for family adventure, including cabins, a lodge, covered docks, and houseboat, pontoon, and fishing boat rentals. To find out more, call (706) 276–4891.

Once families have explored the north Georgia mountains, children begin to understand that all Native Americans didn't live in tepees. They're astonished, however, with the magnificent two-story Federal-style brick home of Chief James Vann, a significant Cherokee chief. The **Chief Vann House Historic Site** (82 US 225) contains not only the original log cabin in which he lived but also the "Showplace of the Cherokee Nation" that he built in 1804. The first mansion ever built by a Native American, the house is furnished with antiques appropriate to the period and features a superb cantilevered stairway and woodwork carved with Cherokee roses (Georgia's state flower). At one time the house was called Diamond Hill and served as the center of a large, prosperous plantation complete with mills, ferries, taverns, and even slaves. It was also a tribal meeting place and a site where Native Americans met with Moravian missionaries. Vann, although controversial, is credited with bringing education to the Cherokee. The site is open from 9:00 A.M. to 5:00 P.M. Tuesday through Saturday and from 2:00 to 5:30 P.M. on Sunday; it is closed Mondays, Thanks-giving, and Christmas. To learn more, call (706) 695–2598.

For the truly adventurous family, the 34,000 acres of the Chattahoochee National Forest known as the **Cohutta Wilderness** are accessible only by footpath. Not only does the wilderness contain the southern end of the Appalachian Mountain chain, it also embraces the Conasauga and Jacks Rivers—two of the best wild trout streams in Georgia. Accessible off US 411, the wilderness is ideal for serious backpackers. For more information, contact the U.S. Forest Service at (706) 695–6736.

If you're looking for an ideal family resort, try the **Cohutta Lodge** (500 Cochise Trail) high atop Fort Mountain. The lodge provides accommodations and a restaurant with a sweeping view of the mountain. Horseback riding is a popular activity. The lodge and restaurant are open year-round. To find out more or to make reservations, call (706) 695–9601.

Inquisitive people of all ages are engrossed by an ancient mountaintop fortification believed to have been built by Native Americans more than 1,000 years ago. The mysterious wall is just one of the attractions at **Fort Mountain State Park** on State 52. Generally considered to be the terminus of the Blue Ridge Mountains with an elevation more than 2,800 feet, the park offers a lake with a beach as well as outdoor activities such as fishing, pedal boat rentals, and hiking trails. Accommodations are available in tent and trailer sites or in cottages. The park is open daily from 7:00 A.M. to 10:00 P.M. To learn more, call (706) 695–2621.

ELLIJAY

Ellijay is the Apple Capital of Georgia, as well as one of the gateways to Carter's Lake and a popular launching site for white-water canoeing and kayaking. When you want fresh apples, this is the place to go. Apple houses begin to open in late summer and remain open through December. Some orchards allow your family the pleasurable experience of picking your own fruit. For information on a wealth of activities available in the area, contact the Gilmer County chamber of commerce at (706) 635–7400.

A tradition for twenty-five years, the **Georgia Apple Festival/Arts and Crafts Fair**, held for two October weekends at the Lions Club Fairgrounds, spotlights foods featuring apples, but also offers more than 200 arts and crafts vendors, live entertainment, and a special children's section. To learn more about the festival, call (706) 636–4500.

JASPER

Marble sculptures and a tour of the Georgia Marble Company and its mine—the world's largest open-pit marble quarry—are the stars of the **Georgia Marble Festival** held in early October in Jasper Park, but also on tap are such child-pleasing activities as a vintage car show and an aircraft exhibit, as well as arts and crafts. Reservations for the tour are suggested. To find out more, call (706) 692–5600.

Show children how the old stone-ground method was used to turn grain into meal at **John's Mill,** a water-run mill on the banks of the Scarecorn Creek at Talking Rock. The picturesque setting includes a stone dam and wooden flume. Freshly ground meal is for sale. The mill is open and operating on weekends from sunrise to sunset. To learn more about the mill, call (706) 692–5600.

CALHOUN

Don't forget your camera when you go to see this live history lesson. The Civil War **Battle of Resaca** is reenacted the third weekend each May on a tract of land at exit 132 off I-75 between Calhoun and Resaca. Visitors are encouraged to question the hundreds of authentically costumed soldiers who set up camp on the grounds. For more information, call (706) 625–3200.

No wonder **Hidden Lake** in the **Chattahoochee National Forest** got labeled with this name. The stream appears and runs clear and cold for a few days, then disappears again only to come to light again who knows when. Truly off the beaten path, the Hidden Creek Recreational Area, on Forest Service Road 228, provides chances for camping, picnicking, and hiking. The recreation area is open during daylight hours for hiking and picnicking. To learn more, call the forest supervisor at (770) 536–0541.

Children love airplanes and they can get up close and personal with some of them at the **Mercer Air Museum** at Mercer Marine Transit on Belwood Road at exit 129 off I–75. An open-air display of seventeen aircraft dating from 1944 can be examined daily during daylight hours. To find out more, call (706) 629–7371.

Once Native Americans tilled the fields in the area now known as Calhoun and established a village here. Now you can follow in their footsteps as you explore the **New Echota State Historic Site** (State 225), which from 1825 to 1838 served as the last Capital of the Cherokee nation. An independent nation that covered north Georgia and parts of four other southeastern states, New Echota is the place in which the Cherokees used the Sequoyah syllabary, the Cherokee alphabet, to produce *The Cherokee Phoenix*, the first Native American newspaper ever printed in North America. In 1838 the Cherokee Indians were rounded up and removed to Oklahoma on the "Trail of Tears." After this lamentable removal of the Cherokee, the village completely disappeared, but today reconstructed buildings allow you to see how they lived. Rather than the stereotypical Indian village, New Echota was a traditional American town of frame homes and farm buildings, a newspaper printing office, and a tavern. The council house, which could just as well have been a courthouse in any southern town, also served as a school. The visitor center offers a film about the site and houses an interpretive museum. Special events throughout the year include living history demonstrations. The site is open 9:00 A.M. to 5:00 P.M. Tuesday through Saturday and 2:00 to 5:30 P.M. Sunday. It is closed Mondays, Thanksgiving, and Christmas. To learn more about New Echota, call (706) 629–8151.

Revisit Civil War history at **Oakleigh** (335 South Wall Street), once the headquarters of Union General William T. Sherman on his push to Atlanta and now home of the Gordon County Historical Society. The home is open Monday through Friday from 10:00 A.M. to 4:00 P.M. Call (706) 629–1515.

Pack a picnic and take the family for an outing at **Salacoa Creek Park** (east of Calhoun on State 156), a 343-acre recreational area with a 126-acre lake. Boating is permitted, but only with electric motors. Other family-pleasing activities include fishing, swimming, picnicking, camping, and an annual bass tournament. The park is open Memorial Day to Labor Day from 7:00 A.M. to 8:00 P.M. From the first Saturday in March to Memorial Day and from Labor Day to the end of October, it is open weekends only from 7:00 A.M. to 8:00 P.M. For more information, call (706) 629–3490.

Free programs varying from astronomy to nature study attract families to the **Sunrise Planetarium,** located on State 53, west of Calhoun. Programs are presented every Sunday afternoon at 3:00 P.M. Camp Sunrise is offered in the summer. To learn more, call (706) 337–2775.

SUMMERVILLE

Everyone can have fun at **James H. "Sloppy" Floyd State Park** (US 27), a small, delightful day-use recreational area and campground that is particularly popular for fishing. Named for one of the most colorful statesmen in Georgia's history, the 35-acre park contains two managed fishing lakes, tent and trailer sites, electric-powered boat rental, pedal boats, playgrounds, and picnicking areas, but no swimming. The park is open daily from 7:00 A.M. to 10:00 P.M. To find out more, call (706) 857–5211.

Famous folk artist Howard Finster has a vision all his own. Budding artists can experience his unique creations at **Paradise Gardens,** Rina and Lewis streets, three blocks off US 27 north of Summerville. A maze of abstract, surreal, bizarre sculptures, paintings, and structures, most of the art works contain a spiritual homily. The artist's property is open from 10:00 A.M. to 6:00 P.M. daily. Call (706) 857–2926.

ROME

Native American residents called the region *Chiaha* or "meeting of the hills and rivers." Early settlers to the area of seven hills noted the similarity to Rome, Italy, and so the town was named in its honor. In recognition of that distinction, the European city presented a replica of the Etruscan Wolf Statue to its American counterpart. Founded in 1834, Rome quickly became a thriving commercial center. Today the city boasts nine historic districts.

Begin a family visit to the town with a stop at the **Rome Welcome Center**, located in a restored 1901 railroad depot and caboose on Civic Center Hill. Children can explore the red caboose and the adjacent 1850 log cabin. From the welcome center you can rent an audiotape that accompanies a walking/driving tour with descriptions of the city's attractions and its significance in north Georgia's history. While you're touring the city be sure to point out the beautiful clock tower to the children, who will be amazed to find out that it really contains the town's water supply. The welcome center is open Monday through Friday from 9:00 A.M. to 5:00 P.M., Saturday from 10:00 A.M. to 3:00 P.M., and Sunday from noon to 3:00 P.M. It is closed on major holidays. For more information, call (800) 444-1834.

The family can learn more about Native American history at the **Chieftains Museum** (501 Riverside Parkway), housed in the 1794 home of Major Ridge, another important Cherokee leader and one of the signers of the Treaty of New Echota. Major Ridge struggled to adapt to white men's ways, mediated disputes with other tribes, and earned his rank at the Battle of Horseshoe Bend in Alabama. He and his family were ferryboat masters, storekeepers, and slave-holding planters. The museum contains exhibits pertaining to Cherokee history, Ridge's life, and the chronicles of the area. It is open Tuesday through Friday from 10:00 A.M. to 4:00 P.M., Sunday from 1:00 to 4:00 P.M., or by appointment. To learn more, call (706) 291-9494.

You can relive the gracious antebellum era at **Oakhill** (US 27 at State Loop 1), which was the 1847 plantation home of Martha Berry, founder of Berry College. Tour the white-columned 1847 home—now the **Martha Berry Museum and Art Gallery**—then stroll around the manicured lawns, through the formal gardens, and along the nature trails. Kids will especially enjoy the collection of antique carriages and cars in the adjacent carriage house. The house/museum is open Tuesday through Saturday from 10:00 A.M. to 5:00 P.M. and Sunday from 1:00 to 5:00 P.M. For more information, call (706) 291-1883.

What a treat it will be for you and your family to explore the 26,000-

acre campus of **Berry College** (US 27 at State Loop 1). The largest as well as one of the most beautiful college campuses in the world, its landmarks include the Gothic-style Ford Quadrangle buildings (a gift of Mr. and Mrs. Henry Ford), one of the world's largest overshot waterwheels, the Normandy Dairy Barns, and Possum Trot—the 1850 cabin where Berry taught her first lessons. To learn more, call (706) 232-5374.

CAVE SPRING

The town of Cave Spring was named for a huge limestone cavern and the pure natural spring that flows from it. Considered to have medicinal properties, the waters drew many visitors to the small town at the turn of the century. Legend says that Native Americans first discovered the spring and held tribal meetings and competitions near the cave. During the summer children delight in venturing into the cave, reputed to be 300,000 years old. Located in **Rolater Park,** the cave features impressive stalagmites. Excess water from the spring flows into a Georgia-shaped, spring-filled swimming pool—the second-largest pool in the state. Significant buildings in the park include a church built in 1851, a classroom building left from the former Cave Spring Manual Labor School (later the Hearn Academy), and the 150-year-old **Hearn Academy Inn**—now a bed-and-breakfast located in what used to be the school's dormitory. Cave Spring has ninety homes listed on the National Register of Historic Places and is filled with quaint antique and gift shops. Rolater Park is open from 7:00 A.M. to 9:00 P.M. daily. To find out more about the town and park, call (706) 777-3382. For information on the inn, call (706) 777-8865.

CARTERSVILLE

Aircraft, including bombers, trainers, and search-and-attack planes, bring joy and delight to children who explore the outdoor exhibits at the **Air Acres Museum**, located at the Cartersville–Bartow County Airport. The outdoor museum is open Monday through Friday from 9:00 A.M. to 5:00 P.M. To find out more, call (770) 382-7030.

    Allatoona Dam (off I–75 at exit 125) impounds the Etowah River into **Lake Allatoona**, which has 12,000 acres and 270 miles of shoreline.

A perfect place for a day's escape for the family, the lake and its thirty-six public use areas offer numerous outdoor and water sports activities. Long before there was a lake, Native Americans lived in the area. Later miners extracted precious ores from beneath the ground. Children can investigate both these historic periods and others at the visitor center atop the dam, where a film and exhibits interpret the natural and cultural history of Bartow County and of the lake. The visitor center is open daily from 8:00 A.M. to 6:00 P.M. For more information, call (770) 382–4700.

A history lesson for the entire family can be had by making a stop at the **Bartow History Center** at 319 East Cherokee Avenue. Exhibits on Northwest Georgia's culture, industry, trade, politics, transportation, and agriculture are all on display at the museum. Young visitors are treated to a glimpse of workshops, farmsteads, and the mercantile trade. The museum is open Tuesday through Saturday from 10:00 A.M. to 4:00 P.M. To find out more, call (770) 382–3818.

Ancient Mississippian Native Americans occupied northwest Georgia between A.D. 1000 and 1500. Travel back in time to that culture by visiting the **Etowah Indian Mounds** (813 Indian Mounds Road), which are gigantic remnants of that society. These mounds comprise one of the most intact Mississippian sites in the East. Although you'll want to see the video presentation and explore the interpretive museum to learn more about the Mississippian civilization, the biggest treat for children is climbing to the flat tops of the three major ceremonial mounds. In fact, they'll probably want to race you to the top up the wooden stairways that protect the slopes. The mounds and interpretive center are open Tuesday through Saturday from 9:00 A.M. to 5:00 P.M. and Sunday from 2:00 to 5:30 P.M. The site is closed on Mondays except those included in a holiday weekend. For more information, call (770) 387–3747.

Children not familiar with old-fashioned "kissing" bridges enjoy a stop at **Lowery Covered Bridge**—also known as the Euharlee Creek Bridge—on State 113. The oldest covered bridge in Georgia, it was constructed using the lattice design. Assembled elsewhere to assure a perfect fit and then disassembled, the bridge was finally reconstructed over the stream.

Those curious about the turn-of-century Southern black experience should visit **Noble Hill** at 2361 Joe Frank Harris Parkway. The black history museum and cultural center is housed in the former Noble Hill Rosenwald School. Built in 1923, it was the first school in northwest Georgia constructed with Rosenwald funds for the education of black children. Among the exhibits are artifacts such as kettles, washboards, desks, and wooden carvings, as well as old pictures of the first principal and first teacher. The school museum is open Tuesday through Friday from 8:00 A.M. to 4:00 P.M. For more information, call (770) 382–3392.

A great spot for a family adventure, **Red Top Mountain State Park** on 653 Red Top Mountain Road offers 1,950 acres of nature and recreation, as well as cottages and a lodge with a restaurant. Named for Georgia's red, iron-rich soil, this park is one of the state's most visited. Located on a wooded peninsula overlooking Lake Allatoona, Red Top is a haven for nature lovers and wildlife observers, as well as for campers, anglers, and hikers. The park is open daily from 7:00 A.M. to 10:00 P.M. To learn more or make reservations, call (770) 975–0055.

Rock hounds can spend hours in the **William Weinman Mineral Museum** (US 411) examining rocks, minerals, fossils, and gemstones from northwest Georgia, the Southeast, and all over the world. Another highlight sure to tickle the fancy of youngsters is an artificial cave. The museum sponsors a **Rock Swap and Festival** the second weekend in June. You can visit the museum Tuesday through Saturday from 10:00 A.M. to 4:30 P.M. and Sunday from 2:00 to 4:30 P.M. To find out more, call (770) 386–0576.

ADAIRSVILLE

In the early 1800s, Godfrey Barnsley carved an estate with formal gardens out of the wilderness. The family was deeply involved in the Civil War and a skirmish occurred on the property; the house, however, was spared. After the war, declining family fortunes continued unabated, and by the turn of the century, the mansion and gardens were in ruins. Recently resurrected, **Barnsley Gardens,** at 597 Barnsley Gardens Road, provides a relaxing family outing. Children can play hide and seek in the ruin of the mansion and examine the exhibits in a small museum contained in the one surviving wing of the house. Then they can skip through the nature trails that wind through the numerous formal and informal gardens. Take a picnic and enjoy it on the shores of a pond, in a meadow, or in an orchard.

Alternatively, you can have lunch in the restaurant housed in a historic house that was restored and moved to the gardens. In addition, there's a gift shop and a garden shop. Many special events are held throughout the year. The gardens are open Tuesday through Sunday from 10:00 A.M. to 6:00 P.M. They are closed Mondays and the month of January. To learn more, call (770) 773–7480.

One of the most colorful incidents during the Civil War was the Great Locomotive Chase, which has been immortalized in two movies. A group of daring Yankees infiltrated the South and hijacked a train pulled by the locomotive *The General.* Determined Southerners chased the train in a series of trains; the last one—*The Texas*—was commandeered in Adairsville. Although the Southerners were ultimately successful in catching the train and the hijackers, the Yankees were later awarded this nation's first Congressional Medals of Honor. The riveting historical event is commemorated the first weekend of October with the **Great Locomotive Chase Festival,** which features an exotic animal show, a gunfight, singing groups, cloggers, more than 100 booths, a cake walk, and demonstrations of pioneer skills such as soapmaking. The Friday of the festival weekend is kiddie day, with activities geared to small fry. For more information, call City Hall at (770) 773–3451.

Stop for lunch at the **1902 Stock Exchange** at 124 Public Square; then wander around the emporium perusing the antiques, arts and crafts, and new and used books. Create a family memory that you can take home with you by dressing up in vintage clothing and having a portrait taken. Dinner theater productions revolving around the history of the area are offered periodically. The store is open Tuesday through Sunday from 10:00 A.M. to 5:00 P.M. For more information about the 1902 Stock Exchange or for a schedule of performances, call (770) 773–1902.

ALPHARETTA

Tucked away on the edge of the metropolitan area, the **Autrey Mill Nature Preserve** (9770 Autrey Mill Road) provides a welcome respite from fast-paced city life. Wildlife and natural scenic beauty combine with the ruins of Autrey Mill and Dam, which dates back to the 1800s, as well as several historic farm buildings to transport you to a simpler time. During the summer months, the buildings are open from 9:00 A.M. to 5:00 P.M. on weekends; the remainder of the year they are open during special monthly programs. The grounds are accessible during daylight hours seven days a week. To find out more about the park or for a schedule of events, call (770) 664–0660.

Aspiring chefs among the youngsters in your group can brush up on their skills with cooking classes designed just for them at the **Kroger School of Cooking** (12460 Crabapple Road), the brainchild of Chef Bernard Kinsella, who began his own career at age ten. Classes, which include student participation, are geared for ages six through nine and ages eleven through thirteen. While teaching fun ways to prepare nutritious foods, Chef Bernard directs tasty assignments that range from creating basic pretzels to making fruit-filled pancakes. Make sure the youngsters go to class hungry—part of the fun is sampling the finished products. Call the cooking school at (770) 740–2068 for a schedule of classes.

Your family doesn't have to venture into the wilds of northern Georgia to experience canoeing and rock climbing. In fact, you can take paddling lessons on the Chattahoochee River at the **Providence Outdoor Recreation Center** at 13313 Providence Road. In addition, day trips are scheduled one Saturday per month; other weekend and/or weekday trips can be arranged. The center provides canoe rentals and shuttle transport. Adventurous souls in your family can sharpen up their rock climbing or rapelling skills at the rock quarry on the property. The grounds are accessible daily during daylight hours. To learn more about scheduled activities, call (770) 740–2419.

If you have horse lovers in your family, they'll be thrilled with the numerous equestrian events that take place almost every weekend at the **Wills Park Equestrian Center**, at 11915 Wills Road. Outdoor and covered show rings set the stage for Western and English events such as rodeos and dressage competitions. Wander around the 300 stalls that house the visiting horses. Getting to know both the steeds and their owners is a pleasure. For a schedule of events, call (770) 740–2400.

DULUTH

All aboard! Railroad buffs can wander around and through acres of restored and unrestored railway cars, tracks, signals, and engines at the **Southeast Railway Museum** at 3966 Buford Highway. Curious children and adults can watch cars and engines undergoing restoration at the complex operated and maintained by the Atlanta Chapter of the National Railway Historical Society. You can hop on board for a train ride around the property on the third weekend each month. The train ride is included in the price of admission. The outdoor museum is open Saturdays from 9:00 A.M. to 5:00 P.M. and Sunday from noon to 5:00 P.M. To learn more, call (770) 476–2013.

ROSWELL

Roswell was one of the only towns near Atlanta that didn't suffer major damage during the Atlanta Campaign of the Civil War. This charming Southern town has several historic districts dating from 1839. Begin your tour with a visit to the **Roswell Convention and Visitors Bureau** at 617 Atlanta Street across from the Town Square. Pick up a brochure for a self-guided walking or driving tour past two dozen historic sites. Guided tours are offered by the Roswell Historical Society on Wednesdays at 10:00 A.M. and Saturdays at 11:00 A.M. The welcome center is open Monday through Friday from 9:00 A.M. to 5:00 P.M., Saturday from 10:00 A.M. to 4:00 P.M., and Sunday from noon to 3:00 P.M. For more information, call (770) 640–3253.

An oasis of antebellum life located in the midst of bustling modern life is the **Archibald Smith Plantation House** at 935 Alpharetta Street. Once isolated at the edge of town, the plantation has gradually been swallowed up by Roswell's phenomenal growth. Start your family's journey into the past by touring the house, which was the home of one of Roswell's founders. Smith family members lived there until only a few years ago, so the landmark is well preserved, unaltered, and filled with antiques and original memorabilia. After touring the house, investigate the intact collection of outbuildings, including a detached kitchen, slave cabin, corn crib, and other farm structures. The historic house and grounds are open Tuesday through Saturday from 11:00 A.M. to 2:00 P.M. To learn more, call (770) 992–1665.

In contrast to the relatively plain Archibald Smith Plantation House, **Bulloch Hall** at 180 Bulloch Avenue is a grand antebellum Greek Revival mansion that was the home of Theodore Roosevelt's mother, Mittie

Bulloch; she was also the grandmother of Eleanor Roosevelt. Costumed guides regale you with anecdotes about the house, the family, and its most famous visitor, Theodore Roosevelt. One of the bedrooms, known as Mittie's Room, is furnished as it would have been when Roosevelt's mother lived there. You'll also be fascinated by the Bulloch/Roosevelt family mementos and Civil War artifacts displayed in the Museum Room. Both you and the children will be even more intrigued, however, if you can schedule a visit when the Open Hearth Guild is giving demonstrations of fireplace cooking or when the weaving or quilting guilds are working on their projects. Demonstrations of nineteenth-century skills and crafts are often given, and numerous classes are scheduled year-round. The house is open Monday through Friday from 10:00 A.M. to 3:00 P.M. and on weekends during special events. For more information about touring the house or for schedules of special events or classes, call (770) 992–1731.

The attractions at the **Chattahoochee Nature Center** (9135 Willeo Road) keep your family busy studying Mother Nature, whose wonders are on display there. Observation points overlook a pond filled with fish, ducks, and turtles; nature trails meander through the heavily wooded property; and a scenic boardwalk allows you to wander over the marshlands of the Chattahoochee River. The Natural Science Education Center offers a Bird of Prey Rehabilitation program. The gift shop is crammed with books on nature, bird feeders, and other nature-related products. Year-round you'll find a wide variety of classes and special events. The nature center is open Monday through Saturday from 9:00 A.M. to 5:00 P.M. and Sunday from noon to 5:00 P.M. To learn more, call (770) 992–2055.

In a survey of parents by *Atlanta Parents* magazine, **Hobbit Hall** at 120 Bulloch Avenue was named the most preferred children's book store in the metropolitan Atlanta area. Even though both parents and children like the wide selection of books, what really lights up the eyes of tiny tots are the storytelling sessions that are scheduled at 10:00 A.M. on Monday, Tuesday, and Saturday. The bookstore is open Monday through Saturday 10:00 A.M. to 6:00 P.M. and Sunday from 1:00 to 5:00 P.M. Call (770) 587–0907 for more information.

Because **Roswell Mill** produced gray fabric for Confederate uniforms during the Civil War, it was a prime target for Union forces. After the mill

Gather around, relax in the shade, and enjoy a good story at Bulloch Hall in Roswell.

was destroyed, the women and children who had been left to operate it while the men were off fighting were shipped north and were never heard from again—one of the unsolved mysteries of the Civil War. A new mill soon replaced the old one and operated until the 1950s. Once it closed the mill was devoured by kudzu until it was rescued, renovated, and reincarnated for quaint gift shops, a variety of restaurants, and several trendy nightspots. Special events take place at the mill year-round, including an outdoor concert series during the summer. In general the stores are open daily from 9:00 A.M. to 6:00 P.M., and the restaurants and nightspots are open until late evening or even into the wee hours of the morning. To learn more or for a schedule of events, including the summer concert series, call (770) 642–6140.

Children may protest that they'd never set foot in a school if they didn't have to, but here's one they'll visit gladly. Located in a former school, the **Teaching Museum—North** (791 Mimosa Boulevard) houses not only exhibits and visual displays of political, social, and historical significance to Roswell and the surrounding area but also contains the Writer's Corner, the Court's Revival, a storyteller's corner, and a Toy Attic. It's best to make an appointment to see the museum or to call ahead to make sure someone is there. To learn more, call (770) 552–6339.

One of metropolitan Atlanta's best-kept secrets is the **Vickery Creek Unit** of the **Chattahoochee National Recreation Area**. Accessed off Riverside Drive, the park is an ideal place for an active family to spend the day. The topography in the heavily wooded park includes steep cliffs, rugged rocky outcroppings, and level terrain along stream banks, resulting in 11.5 miles of hiking trails of varying degrees of difficulty. In addition, the park provides opportunities for fishing, rock climbing, and picnicking, as well as exploring the historic 1860s mill dam and several mill ruins. The park is open from one-half hour after sunrise to one-half hour after sunset. For more information, call (770) 399–8070.

MARIETTA/COBB

American Adventures (exit 113 off I–75), is a theme park created to resemble a turn-of-the-century park. Family-oriented entertainment suitable for all ages, including younger children, includes go-cart racing, miniature golf, bumper cars, a mini roller coaster, a carousel, a children's play area, a restaurant, an arcade, and more. The amusement park is open daily from 10:00 A.M. to 6:00 P.M. from Memorial Day to Labor Day. To find out more, call (770) 424–9283.

The current popularity of the book *The Bridges of Madison County* and the movie based on it has resurrected an appreciation for covered bridges. **Concord Bridge** on Concord Road off South Cobb Drive in the southern part of the county is a 133-foot Queenpost-design covered bridge built in 1848.

With rides from mild to wild in its eight themed sections on 331 acres, **Six Flags Over Georgia** on I–20 is the Southeast's premier amusement park. In addition to enough heart-pounding rides to please any thrill seeker, there are plenty of activities for children of all ages to try. Six Flags also offers shows, performances such as a country music show, a 1950s theme show, fireworks, light shows, a Batman stunt show, and national entertainers at the amphitheater, as well as games, food, and shopping. The amusement park is open daily from Memorial Day through August between 10:00 A.M. and 9:00 P.M. with evening hours extended to midnight on Friday and Saturday. The park is open weekends only from mid-March through Memorial Day and in September and October. For more information, call (770) 948–9290.

For the aquatically inclined, **White Water** (250 North Cobb Parkway) is the ultimate in water theme parks. Named the most scenic water park in the nation, the complex offers forty attractions ranging from relaxing to high-thrill. Tree-shaded waterfalls, lazy rivers, family raft rides, the four-story Tree House Island, and Atlanta's only ocean are among the options. White Water is open daily from Memorial Day through Labor Day between 10:00 A.M. and 9:00 P.M. with evening hours extended to 10:00 P.M. on Friday and Saturday. It is open weekends only in May. To find out more, call (770) 424–WAVE (9283).

KENNESAW

A Civil War occurrence that legends are made of was the abduction of a train from Big Shanty by Union spies. The resultant Great Locomotive Chase (see Adairsville on page 79) involved several other trains and culminated in the capture of the instigators. That wasn't the end of

Kennesaw's involvement in the Civil War. In 1864 Confederate soldiers held off Union troops for several weeks at Kennesaw Mountain.

Relive the Great Locomotive Chase at the **Big Shanty Museum** (2829 Cherokee Avenue), where a film describes the entire incident. Seeing the famous abducted engine *The General* and examining the numerous Civil War artifacts can keep the family engrossed for hours. The museum is open from 9:30 A.M. to 5:30 P.M. Monday through Saturday and from noon to 5:30 P.M. on Sunday. For more information, call (770) 428–6039.

Confederate soldiers kept the Union at bay for weeks at **Kennesaw Mountain National Battlefield Park** at 900 Kennesaw National Drive. At the park, which commemorates the momentous battle, an interpretive museum offers exhibits and a slide presentation about the conflict. Energetic families can hike up the mountain by way of paved trails that pass the well-preserved remains of breastworks. On weekends the less energetic can ride a shuttle bus almost to the summit, then walk the rest of the way. Numerous cannons and historic markers line the route. From the peak, on a clear day you can get a panoramic view of downtown Atlanta. The park, which also offers several picnicking areas, is open daily

The numerous cannons at Kennesaw Mountain National Battlefield Park will intrigue children of all ages.

from 8:30 A.M. to 5:00 P.M. except Christmas Day. Evening hours are extended in the summer. To learn more, call (770) 427–4686.

DALLAS

If your family thirsts for more Civil War history, **Pickett's Mill Historic Site** (2640 Mountain Tabor Road) is among the best-preserved Civil War battlefields in the country. Hiking trails permit visitors to view the surviving breastworks. The interpretive center features exhibits and a film about the battle that was one of the Confederacy's most dramatic victories. Your family will learn a lot from the living history programs that are presented the first and third weekend of each month. The historic site is open from 9:00 A.M. to 5:00 P.M. Tuesday through Saturday and from 2:00 to 5:30 P.M. on Sunday. It is closed Mondays, Thanksgiving, and Christmas. To find out more, call (770) 443–7850.

Racing thrills and excitement can be yours at the **Southeastern International Dragway** (1653 Dragstrip Road), where races are held every Saturday night between April and October on the 8-mile drag racing track. For more information or a schedule of events, call (770) 445–2183.

VILLA RICA

Here's an idea for a vacation that will have your family eager to pack and get going: **Twin Oaks Bed and Breakfast and Farm Vacations** at 9565 East Liberty Road offers you the chance to stay in a plush private cottage on a twenty-three-acre farm while getting to know the farm menagerie, which includes swans, ostriches, mallards, Chinese and Egyptian geese, turkeys, rabbits, chickens, and a fair number of cats and dogs that ramble about unfettered. Fish in the farm pond and swim in the pool with a water slide. To learn more or to make reservations, call (770) 459–4374.

POWDER SPRINGS

Spend a fun-filled day at **Sun Valley Beach** (5350 Holloman Road), which has not only the largest swimming pool in the Southeast, but also offers fourteen water slides, volleyball, go-carts, baseball, basketball, and picnic grounds. The complex is open from May 1 through Labor Day from 10:00

A.M. to 8:00 P.M. daily. A child-care program offered from Memorial Day to Labor Day makes the park even more popular with families. To learn more, call (770) 943–5900.

LITHIA SPRINGS

Combine a history lesson with outdoor activities at **Sweetwater Creek State Conservation Park** on Mount Vernon Road. The ruin on the grounds was a Civil War textile mill. Activities for the sports-minded include canoe rentals, fishing, and hiking. Picnicking areas help you enjoy the natural beauty of the park, which is open from 7:00 A.M. to 10:00 P.M. daily. To learn more, call (770) 944–1700.

The rare metal lithium, hailed by doctors in the nineteenth century for its curative properties, is found in only four springs in the world. One of them is western Georgia's **Lithia Springs**. This singular water is still bottled by **Lithia Springs Water and Bottling Company** at 2910 Bankhead Highway. Children examine Indian artifacts as well as see some turn-of-the-century medical paraphernalia at the company's museum. Out of doors, you can wander through a garden cultivated with plants that have medicinal value. Children may be surprised to learn that other forms of medicine exist beyond pills, syrups, and shots. Make sure to point out to the children the Frog Rock—a natural oddity that resembles an American bullfrog. The museum is open Monday through Friday from 9:00 A.M. to 4:00 P.M.; the gardens are accessible during daylight hours. For more information, call (770) 944–3880.

ATLANTA METRO

Atlanta, Capital of the New South, is on the fast track. Not only is the city home to Coca-Cola, the world's most popular soft drink, and Cable News Network, but its airport is one of the busiest in the country. The city hosted the 1994 Super Bowl and will welcome the world to the 1996 Summer Olympic Games. Atlanta is a popular tourism city and the number two convention spot in the country—a vibrant city that abounds in family attractions ranging from simple diversions to highly sophisticated entertainment. We suggest beginning a visit with a guided tour such as those offered by

Gray Line of Atlanta (404–767–0594). Such a tour will orient you to the city and its attractions, after which you can plan what you want to see in more detail. The best way to get around in Atlanta is via the trains and buses of the Metropolitan Atlanta Rapid Transit Authority (MARTA). The transportation system includes 1,500 miles of bus routes and 39 miles of rapid rail lines. Many of the attractions listed below are accessible by MARTA bus and/or rail, as is Atlanta Hartsfield International Airport. Provisions are made on the last car of each train for transporting bicycles. For more information, route maps, and schedules, call (404) 848–4711. Two tourist cards are good for discounts all around the city. For more information about the Atlanta Metro Travel and Discount Card, call (800) ATLANTA; for the DeKalb–Atlanta Guest Card, call (800) 999–6065, extension 1203. For your ease in finding an Atlanta attraction, we've departed from our normal alphabetical format and instead have arranged attractions and activities by category.

Atlanta abounds with entertainment options for fun-loving families. Sample some of the following opportunities.

Get your children accustomed to being theater-goers early in life by taking them to performances at the **Alliance Children's Theater** at 1280 Peachtree Street NE. The theater company prepares two plays each year, such as the ever-popular *Charlotte's Web*. One of the plays is appropriate for children in grades kindergarten through four and the other is prepared for children in grades four through eight. Although performances are given only for school groups during the week, shows are presented for families on Saturday. In addition, the Alliance Theater Company presents the ever-popular family-oriented *A Christmas Carol* each year from Thanksgiving through Christmas. For a schedule of performances, call (404) 733–4660; for tickets call (404) 733–5000.

The **Atlanta Symphony Orchestra** (Woodruff Arts Center, 1293 Peachtree Street, NE) offers many ways to introduce your children to the world of the symphony. Among the extensive array of classical and pops concerts the symphony performs throughout the year are free summer concerts given in various parks around the city. An excellent way to expose your children to the symphony without requiring them to sit still, these concerts permit you to bring a blanket or lawn chairs and a picnic. Particularly enjoyed by families are the Family Concerts performed at Halloween and Christmas, usually with lots of explanations about the orchestra and its individual instruments and often with visits by popular children's characters. During the summer pops are performed at the Chastain Memorial Park Amphitheater, where concert-goers can dine on elaborate picnic suppers while listening to the orchestra and guest stars by candlelight. To learn more or to get a schedule of concerts, call (404) 892–2414.

A special place for families to enjoy together is the **Center for Puppetry Arts** at 1404 Spring Street. Not only a performance venue, the center has the largest collection of puppets in the world. Children are agog with the tremendous variety of puppets—many kinds of which they may not have even realized existed. A new interactive exhibit is called "Puppets—the Power of Wonder." Youngsters older than three can make their own puppets at periodic puppetry workshops. During the school year, performances are at 10:00 A.M. and 11:30 A.M. on weekdays with an extra performance on Wednesday at 1:00 P.M. and two more performances on Saturday. During the summer festival, performances are at 11:00 A M. and 1:00 P.M. The ticket office is open Monday through Saturday from 9:00 A.M. to 5:00 P.M. Reservations are strongly recommended; many performances sell out quickly. A twenty-four-hour hotline (404) 874–0398 provides general information. For tickets, call the box office at (404) 873–3391.

No matter what your family's interests, you're sure to find one or more of Atlanta's museums fascinating.

The Paul Jones Collection of African-American art is the centerpiece of the displays at the **APEX (African-American Panoramic Experience) Museum** (135 Auburn Avenue, NE), which showcases black history and black artists. The museum is open Tuesday, Thursday, Friday, and Saturday from 10:00 A.M. to 5:00 P.M.; and Wednesday from 10:00 A.M. to 6:00 P.M. During February and the three summer months, the museum is also open on Sundays from 1:00 to 5:00 P.M. For more information, call (404) 521–APEX.

Travel through time at **Atlanta Heritage Row**, located on Upper Alabama Street at Underground Atlanta. This museum describes Atlanta's history from 1838 to the present. An orientation film and the exhibits depict Atlanta's humble beginnings, the era of King Cotton, the devastation of the Civil War, the civil rights movement, and Atlanta's rapid rise to its position as an international city. Children can get involved in events by boarding a trolley or piloting an airplane. The museum is open from 10:00 A.M. to 5:00 P.M. Tuesday through Saturday and from 1:00 to 5:00 P.M. on Sunday. To learn more, call (404) 584–7879.

Get an even more thorough picture of Atlanta's past at the **Atlanta History Center** at 130 West Paces Ferry Road. This complex includes a history museum as well as two historic houses, formal and informal gardens, and acres of woodland. In addition to artifacts from Atlanta's history, the museum displays folk crafts and black history memorabilia, but it is most noted for its extensive collection of Civil War artifacts. Although the adults may appreciate a tour of the 1928 Swan House mansion, an opulent Italianate villa furnished with exquisite antiques and surrounded by gentle terraces and cascading fountains, the children are more likely to enjoy the 1840s Tullie Smith Farm, with a farmhouse and outbuildings where they can learn about such folk sayings as "Sleep tight, don't let the bed bugs bite" and "Whistle while you work." Have a bite to eat at the restaurant and browse through the museum shop. Among many special events throughout the year, the most popular is a Civil War encampment held on the grounds in July. The center is open from 10:00 A.M. to 5:30 P.M. Monday through Saturday and from noon to 5:30 P.M. on Sunday. For more information, call (404) 814–4000.

Many families will never get the opportunity to visit the White House in Washington, D.C., but visitors to the **Carter Presidential Center** (One Copenhill off Freedom Parkway) can see a replica of the presidential Oval Office. The repository of former President Jimmy Carter's library and hundreds of thousands of documents, the museum interprets his life and presidency through numerous exhibits, gifts received during his tenure in the White House, and an interactive town meeting. Hidden to the rear of the building is an exquisite Japanese garden in which you can wander while admiring a splendid vista of the downtown skyline. The center is open Monday through Saturday from 9:00 A.M. to 4:45 P.M. and on Sunday from noon to 4:45 P.M. To find out more, call (404) 331–0296.

Treat your children to a rare sight by visiting the **Cyclorama** in Grant Park at Georgia and Cherokee avenues. The gargantuan 358-foot-by-50-foot circular painting, completed in 1885, is one of only twenty such paintings left in the world. Atlanta's masterpiece depicts the Civil War Battle of Atlanta by using a revolving seating section, a three-dimensional diorama, music, and dramatic lights and sound effects. Also on display are Civil War artifacts and *The Texas*, the legendary locomotive that chased and captured the stolen train *The General* during the war. See the giant painting daily from 9:30 A.M. to 4:30 P.M. between October and May. The remainder of the year, the attraction is open until 5:30 P.M. For more information, call (404) 658–7625.

For an activity both educational and pleasurable, take the children to the **High Museum of Art** at the Woodruff Arts Center at 1280 Peachtree Street, NE. It houses collections of paintings, sculpture, African art, and decorative arts, as well as traveling exhibitions. Inquisitive children are intrigued with all the hands-on activities in the children's discovery center called **Spectacles**. The museum is open Tuesday through Saturday from 10:00 A.M. to 5:00 P.M. with hours extended on Friday to 9:00 P.M., and on Sunday from noon to 5:00 P.M. To learn more, call (404) 733–4200 or the twenty-four-hour Info Line (404) 733–HIGH.

Can there be anything much more fascinating for children than learning about how money is made? Become acquainted with the history of money at the **Monetary Museum** at the Federal Reserve Bank at 104 Marietta Street. Among the displays are gold coins made from north Georgia gold as well as other rare coins. The museum is open Monday through Friday from 9:00 A.M. to 4:00 P.M. To find out more, call (404) 521–8764.

Ask your children—especially the older ones—if they can possibly imagine their lives without a telephone? The thought is horrifying to them. Thankfully, all of you can share in tracing the evolution of this scientific marvel at Southern Bell's **Pioneer Museum**, located on the plaza level of the Southern Bell Center at 675 West Peachtree Street, NE. The first exhibit presents a brief biography of Alexander Graham Bell and describes the significant events leading up to his invention of the telephone. Life-size dioramas include a street scene depicting life in the early twentieth century, as well as a lineman and a switchboard operator at work. Other displays show the evolution of telephone sets from the beginning of World War II; different types of switching equipment; transmission systems including cable, microwave, and satellites; and emergency measures taken during

natural disasters. The museum is open Monday through Friday from 11:00
A.M. to 1:00 P.M. For more information, call (404) 223–3661.

Gone with the Wind buffs can peruse memorabilia from Atlanta's
best-known story at the **Road to Tara Museum** (659 Peachtree Street,
NE/Suite 600) in Atlanta's magnificently restored Georgian Terrace building across the street from the Fox Theater. This is the largest permanent
public collection of such memorabilia anywhere. The museum is open
from 10:00 A.M. to 6:00 P.M. Monday through Saturday and between 1:00
and 6:00 P.M. Sunday. Call (404) 897–1939. ~~405~~
                                        ~~770 - 465~~

Children and adults can experience the excitement of more than 150
hands-on experiments illustrating basic principles of science and their
application to everyday life at **SciTrek, the Science and Technology
Museum of Atlanta** (395 Piedmont Avenue), ranked as one of the top ten
science museums in the country. The museum is open Monday through
Saturday from 10:00 A.M. to 5:00 P.M. and on Sunday from noon to 5:00
P.M. For more information, call (404) 522–5500. 7.00 Adults
                                        5.00 children

A mesmerizing place for the entire family is the **World of Coca-Cola**
at 55 Martin Luther King, Jr. Drive, where you and the kids can examine
more than 1,000 items of memorabilia recounting the one-hundred-year-
plus history of the world's most preferred soft drink. In addition to the
largest collection of Coca-Cola mementoes in existence, the museum's
state-of-the-art video technology shows unforgettable films and commer-
cials. Among the most popular attractions are an old-fashioned soda fountain where you can get a traditional Coke and a futuristic tasting center
where you can sample far-out experimental flavors. The facility is open
Monday through Saturday from 10:00 A.M. to 9:30 P.M. and on Sunday
from noon to 6:00 P.M. The last entry is one hour before closing. The complex is closed on New Year's Day, Easter, Thanksgiving, Christmas Eve, and
Christmas Day. Advance reservations are recommended. Call (404)
676–5151 for more information.

Your exploration of Atlanta is far from complete. A wide range of
attractions offers something for every taste.

No matter what time of year, families are drawn to see the variety of
familiar and unusual flowers and plants blooming at the **Atlanta Botanical
Garden** in Piedmont Park at The Prado. In fact, you'll probably want to

make several trips each year to see what's blooming in different seasons. No matter when you visit you can spend some quiet moments in the serene Japanese Garden or see the tropical and desert habitats in the gigantic glass Dorothy Fuqua Conservatory, where you can also examine endangered plants from around the world. Among the many special yearly programs are some designed especially for children. Between October and March, the garden is open Tuesday through Sunday from 9:00 A.M. to 6:00 P.M.; from April through September, it is open Tuesday through Sunday from 9:00 A.M. to 8:00 P.M. The Conservatory opens at 10:00 A.M. Admission is free on Thursday afternoons after 1:00 P.M. The garden is accessible via MARTA. For information or a schedule of special programs, call (404) 876–5858.

Families are sure to find something interesting at the **Capitol,** Capitol Square downtown. Capped by a dome sheathed in gold from the mines of north Georgia, gorgeous Classic Renaissance-style building houses the **State Museum of Science and Industry,** the **Hall of Flags,** and the **Georgia Hall of Fame.** The Capitol is open Monday through Friday from 8:00 A.M. to 5:00 P.M. Guided tours are given at 10:00 A.M., 11:00 A.M., 1:00 P.M., and 2:00 P.M. To learn more, call (404) 656–2844.

The high-tech, fast-paced, state-of-the-art, twenty-four-hour-a-day Cable News Network and Headline News have changed the face of news broadcasting worldwide. Your family can tour the **CNN Center** on Marietta Street at Techwood Drive and from specially constructed, glass-enclosed overhead walkways can actually watch as up-to-the-minute news events are reported. The center also boasts the Turner Store and the Clubhouse Store. The CNN Center is open from 9:00 A.M. to 5:00 P.M. daily. Call (404) 827–2300 for information.

Take your children on a magic carpet ride to the land of Ali Baba and the forty thieves with a visit to the **Fox Theater** at 660 Peachtree Street, NE. An extravaganza of Art Deco, Moorish, and Egyptian architecture and embellishment completed in 1929, it is one of the most opulent theaters in the country. Tours are given by the Atlanta Preservation Center Monday, Thursday, and Saturday at 10:00 A.M., with an additional tour on Saturday at 11:30 A.M., or by appointment. A full schedule of movie, theatrical, and musical productions are performed year-round, the most popular of which is the summer family movie series. To learn more about the tours, call the Atlanta Preservation Center at (404) 876–2041. To get a schedule of events or to purchase tickets, call the Fox Box Office at (404) 881–2100.

Spend an educational family day at the **Martin Luther King, Jr., National Historic Site** (Auburn Avenue), the most visited attraction in Atlanta. Three sites related to the life of Atlanta native Martin Luther King, Jr. are included: the house where the civil rights leader was born; Ebenezer Baptist Church, where he preached; and the Freedom Hall Complex, which contains the Martin Luther King, Jr., Center for Nonviolent Social Change and the reflecting pool in which Dr. King's burial crypt rests. Begin with the Park Information Office at 522 Auburn Avenue for guided tours. The site is open daily from 9:00 A.M. to 5:30 P.M. During daylight-saving time hours are extended to 8:00 P.M. For more information, call (404) 331–3920 or 524–1956.

Sure to intrigue the children, **Underground Atlanta** at Lower Pryor and Lower Alabama streets is a city beneath the streets encompassing six blocks covering twelve acres of underground and above-ground shopping, restaurants, nightspots, and entertainment. The shops are open Monday through Saturday from 10:00 A.M. to 9:30 P.M. and on Sunday from noon to 6:00 P.M. Hours vary at the restaurants and nightspots, but in general they are open until late evening or into the wee hours. Call (404) 523–2311.

No family should leave Atlanta without chowing down on a hot dog or chili dog accompanied by a mound of onion rings at **The Varsity** at 61 North Avenue NW. Billed as the World's Largest Drive-In, the restaurant has been serving up chili cheese dogs since 1928. You can eat in your car or inside the restaurant. Food is served from 9:30 A.M. to 11:30 P.M. Sunday through Thursday and from 9:30 A.M. to 1:30 A.M. on Friday and Saturday nights. To learn more, call (404) 881–1706.

Today's parents and grandparents grew up on the Uncle Remus stories adapted from old slave tales. Author/journalist Joel Chandler Harris, creator of the stories, lived his adult life in a Victorian home called the **Wren's Nest** at 1050 Ralph David Abernathy Boulevard, SW. Open to the public, the cozy house, furnished with original pieces and Uncle Remus memorabilia, provides a glimpse into the author's family life. Periodic storytelling events re-create the tales for today's children. Be prepared for the youngsters to want some of the books and Br'er Rabbit memorabilia in the gift shop. The house is open Tuesday through Saturday from 10:00 A.M. to 4:00 P.M. and on Sunday from 1:00 to 4:00 P.M. To learn more, call (404) 753-7735.

Take your family on a safari to **Zoo Atlanta** in Grant Park at 800 Cherokee Avenue, SE. Spectacularly improved over the last decade, it is now one of the best zoos in the country—especially noted for its primate collections. More than 900 animals roam freely in natural habitats as diverse as the Arctic tundra and the Asian rainforest. There's an exemplary reptile collection and a petting zoo. In good weather a miniature train chugs around the property carrying small visitors. Among the most popular animals are the gorilla Willie B. and his daughter Kudzu, whose name was chosen in a contest. The "Greatest Baby Elephant Show on Earth" is a guaranteed showstopper. During the summer, you can take the ZOO TROLLEY from the Five Points MARTA station. The zoo is open from 10:00 A.M. to 4:30 P.M. daily. Hours are extended to 5:30 P.M. on summer weekends. To learn more, call (404) 624-5600.

Sports fans, listen up. A team playing almost every major sport calls Atlanta home. The **Atlanta Braves** baseball team plays at Atlanta–Fulton County Stadium, 521 Capitol Avenue (404-249-6400); the **Atlanta Falcons** football team plays at the Georgia Dome, #1 Georgia Dome Drive (404-223-9200); the **Atlanta Hawks** basketball team plays at the Omni Sports Arena, 100 Techwood Drive (404-249-6400); the **Atlanta Knights** hockey team also plays at the Omni Sports Arena (404-420-5000); and the **Atlanta Thunder** professional tennis team plays at the Dixie Crystal Tennis Center Sportslife Club–Cobb, 1775 Water Place (404-881-8811).

More active sports enthusiasts can get into the action in a variety of ways.

As the Chattahoochee River flows from the north Georgia mountains to the Georgia/Florida border, 48 miles of it meander through the metro Atlanta area. Designated as the **Chattahoochee River National Recreation Area**, the fourteen units of the park offer rafting, canoeing, kayaking, rowing, fishing, hiking, mountain biking, horseback riding, and wildlife observation. The most popular unit with families is the Paces Mill segment, which offers raft rentals, a boat launch, and shuttle service. The units are open from one-half hour after sunrise to one-half hour after sunset. To learn more about the entire system, call (770) 394–7912.

Whether you and your family are sports fans or not, everyone will find the architecture of the **Georgia Dome** (One Georgia Dome Drive, NW) awe-inspiring. Public tours of the world's largest cable-supported dome are offered on the hour Tuesday through Saturday 10:00 A.M. to 4:00 P.M. and on Sunday from noon to 4:00 P.M. The dome hosted the 1994 Super Bowl and will be the site of the gymnastics and basketball events during the 1996 Summer Olympic Games. For tour information, call (404) 223–TOUR or 223–8600.

With two locations, there's never a dull moment at these family adventure complexes. **Malibu Grand Prix** provides bumper boats, go-carts, three-fourth-scale Indy cars, miniature golf, batting cages, and an outstanding video arcade. The fun centers are open on weekdays from 11:00 A.M. to 11:00 P.M. and on Fridays and Saturdays from 11:00 A.M. to midnight. The two locations are 400 Brookhollow Parkway, Norcross (770–416–7630) and 3005 George Busbee Parkway, Kennesaw (770–514–8081).

DECATUR

Members of your family can increase their knowledge of the earth sciences at Decatur's **Fernbank Museum of Natural History** (767 Clifton Road), the largest museum of its type in the Southeast. One major exhibit called "A Walk Through Time in Georgia" uses the State of Georgia as a microcosm to tell the story of the earth. The museum contains the state's first IMAX Theater and a dinosaur gallery. Two major children's environments include the Georgia Adventure for six-to-ten-year-olds and the Fantasy Forest for three-to-five-year-olds. The museum is open Monday through Saturday from 10:00 A.M. to 5:00 P.M. with extended hours on Fridays until 9:00 P.M., as well as from noon until 5:00 P.M. on Sunday. For more information, call (404) 378–0127. Another part of the complex is the **Fernbank Science Center** at 156 Heaton Park Drive, NE. It has one of the country's largest planetariums. Also on the grounds are a greenhouse, botanical garden, and a sixty-five-acre forest with paved walking trails—some adapted for heart patients and the visually impaired. Children younger than five years of age are not admitted to the planetarium. Exhibit Hall hours are Monday from 8:30 A.M. to 5:00 P.M., Tuesday through

Friday from 8:30 A.M. to 10:00 P.M., Saturday from 10:00 A.M. to 5:00 P.M., and Sunday from 1:00 to 5:00 P.M. The planetarium shows are Tuesday through Friday at 8:00 P.M., as well as Wednesday and Friday through Sunday at 3:00 P.M. The complex is accessible by MARTA. Call (404) 378–4311 for more information.

Travel back to yesteryear at the **Historic Complex of DeKalb Historical Society,** 720 West Trinity Place, by touring three historic antebellum structures—all built between 1830 and 1840. The Swanton House is Decatur's oldest town house; the Biffle Cabin was built by a Revolutionary War veteran; and the Thomas-Barber Cabin is a hand-hewn log house. Tours of the complex are by appointment. To find out more, call (404) 373–1088.

Introduce your children to ancient world cultures at the **Michael C. Carlos Museum** (Emory University at 571 South Kilgo), the South's largest archaeological museum. See examples of 9,000 years of art and art history: Egyptian mummies; collections of Greek, Near Eastern, and Columbian art; and other ancient artifacts. The museum is open Tuesday through Saturday from 10:00 A.M. to 4:30 P.M. and Sunday from noon to 5:00 P.M. To learn more, call (404) 727–4282.

STONE MOUNTAIN

A family entertainment resort, **Georgia's Stone Mountain Park** on US 78 boasts enough facilities and activities for an afternoon, a day, or a week. The focal point of the park is the world's largest bas-relief sculpture—a rendition of mounted Confederate Civil War heroes Jefferson Davis, Robert E. Lee, and Stonewall Jackson carved on the face of the huge granite mountain. During the summer and on weekends in the fall, the mountain serves as the backdrop for the spectacular Laser Light Show presented nightly. The highlight of the show is when the mounted heroes come to life and circumnavigate the mountain. Other attractions at the 3,200-acre park include a skylift to the top of the mountain, a complete antebellum plantation, a steam-locomotive powered train ride around the mountain, a paddle wheel riverboat, an antique car museum, a Civil War museum, a large lake, an eighteen-hole golf course, a petting zoo, two hotels, camping facilities, and several restaurants. Just a few of the park's many annual special events and festivals include the Antebellum Jubilee, Holiday Celebration, Scottish Festival and Highland Games, Springfest, Taste of the South, and the Yellow Daisy Festival. The gates are open from 6:00 A.M. to midnight. The attractions are open from 10:00 A.M. to 9:00 P.M. from June to August and from 10:00 A.M. to 5:30 P.M. the remainder of the year. Don't miss the laser show given nightly June through September and weekends in May and October. For more information, call (770) 498–5702.

LILBURN

Walk the trails and experience wildlife firsthand at the **Yellow River Wildlife Game Ranch** at 4525 US 78. A unique petting zoo and feeding animal preserve, this is the home of the famous General Beauregard Lee, the groundhog who predicts spring's arrival in the South. After being supplied with food for the animals, visitors walk along a one-mile trail to feed many of the 600 animals that lie in the sprawling twenty-four-acre sanctuary. Concentrating on animals native to Georgia, the zoo boasts animals that range from ferrets to black bears. Some special events include sheep shearing and wilderness hayrides. The animal park is open daily from 9:30 A.M. to 6:00 P.M. from September through May. From Memorial Day to Labor Day, however, it is open from 9:30 A.M. to dusk. For more information, call (770) 972–6643.

JONESBORO

Poke into the past at **Stately Oaks Plantation Home and Historic Community** (100 Carriage Lane) to let your children see what life in Georgia was like more than 150 years ago. The authentic restored home, circa 1839, is surrounded by plantation outbuildings, a one-room school, and a tiny country store that have been moved to the site. The complex is open Thursday and Friday from 11:00 A.M. to 3:00 P.M. and the second and fourth Sundays from 2:00 to 4:00 P.M. Call (770) 473–0197 for more information.

FAIRBURN

Meet Henry VIII and one of his six wives, as well as gallant knights and lovely ladies-in-waiting, peasants and potentates, the Kissing Wench, mud wrestlers, and many other types of sixteenth-century characters at the **Georgia Renaissance Festival.** Located in a field and forest situated at exit 12 off I-85, the village of Willy-Nilly-on-the-Wash comes to life for several weekends in the spring and fall. Watch knights battle it out in a joust. Admire and purchase contemporary and medieval crafts. Become part of the hilarious entertainment and participate in games of the period. Savor typical food and drink such as huge turkey drumsticks, meat pies, sausage on a stick, dill pickles, wine, ale, and lemonade. Every family member enjoys the sights, sounds, smells, and tastes of the fair. To learn more about the festival or to purchase advance tickets, call (770) 964–8575.

WEST POINT

A bonanza for active families, **West Point Lake,** a 25,900-acre lake created by damming the Chattahoochee River, offers excellent fishing and recreational activities. Along the 500 miles of forested shoreline are twenty-seven day-use areas, eleven campgrounds, two marinas, and a 10,000-acre wildlife management area—together providing boating, swimming, fishing, camping, hiking, and hunting. The visitor center and museum located in the Resource Manager's office interprets Native American history and the 1817 battle between the Indians and U.S. soldiers. The center/museum is open Monday through Friday from 8:00 A.M. to 5:30 P.M. and weekends from 9:30 A.M. to 5:30 P.M. between March and September. The remainder of the year, the hours are Monday through Friday 8:00 A.M. to 4:00 P.M. To find out more, call (770) 645–2929.

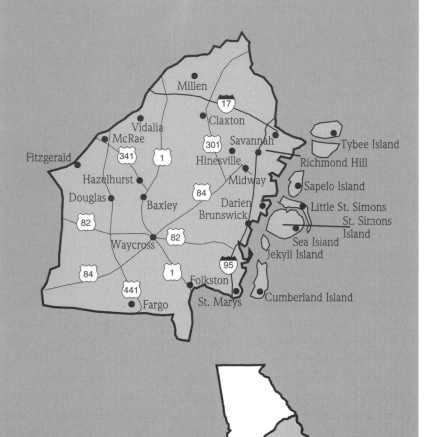

Millen

17

Vidalia • Claxton
McRae •
301 Savannah
Fitzgerald • 341 1 Hinesville Tybee Island
Richmond Hill
Hazelhurst • Midway
Douglas • 84 Sapelo Island
• Baxley Darien Little St. Simons
82 Brunswick St. Simons
Island
82 Sea Island
Waycross • Jekyll Island
84 1 95
Folkston
441 St. Marys
• Fargo Cumberland Island

SOUTHEAST GEORGIA

On the barrier islands, quaint seaside villages dotted with sunny resorts are caressed by soft sea breezes. In complete contrast is the eerie stillness of the dark, brooding primeval Okefenokee Swamp found not too far inland. Gracious Savannah, the Queen City of the South, contains a timeless bounty of architectural treasures. Wherever you go in the state's southeastern corner, life moves at a gentle pace. Families seeking a quiet getaway couldn't make a better choice than to spend considerable time in this bewitching region exploring its profusion of absorbing historical sites, numerous state parks, and breathtaking scenic spots.

MILLEN

A day of outdoor family fun can be yours at **Magnolia Springs State Park** (US 25), which offers camping, cottages, picnicking, fishing, hiking, and a swimming pool and lake. A historic site, the area served as a Civil War prison camp. See the few remains that are left after Union General William Tecumseh Sherman burned the camp. The park is open daily from 7:00 A.M. to 10:00 P.M. For more information, call (912) 982–1660.

VIDALIA

Nowhere in the world are there sweeter onions than those grown in the vicinity of Vidalia. Cotton and tobacco are also important products. Stop by the **Vidalia Welcome Center**, 2805 Lyons Highway, for information about farm tours. Local onion farms, as well as processing and packaging plants are toured in the spring, while cotton and tobacco farms can be toured in the fall. The welcome center is open Monday through Friday from 8:00 A.M. to 5:00 P.M. To learn more about the area or the farm tours or to find out where to buy Vidalia onions, call (912) 538–8687.

CLAXTON

Although fruitcake may not be tops on the children's list of favorite foods, they'll be fascinated to learn that every year six million pounds of the rich cake are baked and distributed internationally from the **Claxton Fruitcake Company** at 203 West Main Street. Although you can tour the bakery by request year-round, the baking season is September through mid-December when it is open Monday through Saturday from 8:00 A.M. to 6:00 P.M. For more information, call (912) 739–3441.

Vanquish the winter blahs with a visit to the **Claxton Rattlesnake Roundup,** held the second weekend in March at the J. Evans County Wildlife Club. Used as a method to thin the rattlesnake population, the roundup is one of the most unusual activities in Georgia. You'll hear plenty of squealing from the young ones (if not from yourself) as all of you watch snake handling and milking the reptiles. To find out more including the exact dates of the next roundup, call (912) 739–2281.

Help your youngsters learn about honey production and pollination at the **Wilbanks Apiary** on US 280W. Tours of this major regional beekeeping operation are by appointment. Afterwards you can purchase honey products to take home. For more information, call (912) 739–4820.

SAVANNAH

Without a doubt each member of your family will surrender to beautiful Savannah's romantic past. Founded in 1733 by General James Oglethorpe and a small group of English settlers, Savannah was the first city in the new colony of Georgia. One of Oglethorpe's most enduring legacies is the careful grid pattern he developed for the city—a pattern broken by twenty-four parklike squares. After 160 years these squares are shaded by gigantic

moss-draped live oaks and magnolias. Lushly landscaped with brilliant azaleas and oleander, the parks feature benches on which to rest while admiring the plantings, fountains, and monuments. Union General William
Tecumseh Sherman captured Savannah in December of 1864, just in time
to present it to Lincoln as a Christmas present. Thankfully, Sherman spared
the city from the destruction he wrought across Georgia. A burst of construction in the late 1800s resulted in the opulent Italianate buildings you
see today. Although many treasures were lost in the 1950s, citizens soon
realized what they were sacrificing. An active preservation movement
resulted in the designation of a 2³⁄₁₀-square- mile National Historic
Landmark District. One of the largest such districts in the country, the area
contains 1,400 historic structures, many of which have been restored to
their former splendor.

Learn about Savannah's history from an audiovisual presentation and
get your bearings to the city's attractions at the **Savannah Visitor Center**
(301 Martin Luther King Boulevard), which is located in a restored 1860s
train station built on the site of the 1779 Siege of Savannah. The visitor
center is open 365 days a year: Monday through Friday from 8:30 A.M. to
5:00 P.M. and weekends from 9:00 A.M. to 5:00 P.M. To find out more, call
(912) 944–0460 or (800) 444–2427.

Delve deeper into Savannah's 260-year history next door in the restored
passenger terminal at the **Savannah History Museum** at 303 Martin Luther
King Boulevard. A fascinating place for those who like history, the museum
offers two theaters that present Savannah's past through films with special
effects, as well as an 1890 steam locomotive, a cotton gin, and artifacts from
Savannah's wars. The museum is open daily including holidays from 8:30
A.M. to 5:00 P.M. For more information, call (912) 238–1779.

Before you leave Savannah's old railroad center, a must-see attraction for
the entire family is the **Central of Georgia Railroad Roundhouse
Complex** (601 West Harris Street), which is one of the largest remaining
pre–Civil War railroad repair and maintenance complexes in the nation.
Among the thirteen original structures are the massive roundhouse and a
125-foot smokestack. Some of the exhibits that get the rapt attention of your
youngsters are two of the oldest surviving steam engines in the country, a
1914 steam locomotive, antique repair machinery, and examples of antiquat-

ed rolling stock. Tours are available Monday, Thursday, and Friday from noon to 4:30 P.M. and weekends from 11:00 A.M. to 4:30 P.M. To learn more, call (912) 238–1414.

Because this is such a historic city, one of the most appropriate ways to see Savannah is via one of the horse-drawn carriages operated by **Carriage Tours of Savannah** at 10 Warner Street. Tours operate daily and evenings from the City Market and the Savannah Visitor Center. To find out more, get a schedule, or make reservations, call (912) 236–6756. Another option is the **Old Town Trolley** at 601 Cohen Street; it also picks up at the Savannah Visitor Center. Call (912) 233–0083 for more information.

The Savannah River is still the heart of the historic district. You'll want to spend some time at **Factor's Walk**, **Old River Street,** and **Riverfront Plaza**—all located along the river. Factor's Walk was the center of commerce when cotton was king. The buildings, which boast opulent iron balconies overlooking the river, housed the factors' (merchants) offices and also served as warehouses. They and the cobblestone streets are reached from Bay Street via ornate iron bridge ways. These buildings now house inns, restaurants, nightspots, and boutiques. Recently spruced up, the waterfront has been transformed into **Riverfront Plaza,** a nine-block brick-paved esplanade dotted with fountains, plantings, and benches. Always a busy place, the plaza is the site of several annual festivals. Make sure to take the children down to the far end of the plaza to see the life-size **Waving Girl Statue,** which salutes Florence Martus. They'll be both intrigued and saddened by her story. Florence's lover, a seaman went off on a voyage and disappeared, but she hopefully greeted every ship that entered the port from 1887 to 1931 anticipating his return.

Above Factor's Walk on the East Bay Street side of the buildings is a narrow tree-shaded park containing several important landmarks. Challenge the children to find the **City Exchange Bell,** the **Washington Guns,** the **Old Harbor Light**, a **fountain** commemorating three famous ships, and a **bench** marking the site where General Oglethorpe landed in 1733.

A paddle wheeler is a perfect way for the family to explore the Savannah River. Climb on board the ***Savannah River Queen,*** operated by the River Street Riverboat Company, located at 9 East River Street. For more information, call (912) 232–6404.

Savannah's parks and forts attract visitors of all ages.

Largest of the parks, **Forsyth Park** at Gaston and Park avenues is a splendid place for a family outing. The site of many annual festivals, the common offers jogging and walking trails, tennis and basketball courts, a fountain dating from 1858, and a fragrance garden for the visually impaired.

Let the youngsters delve into history at **Old Fort Jackson** (1 Fort Jackson Road), the oldest standing fort in Georgia and home of the largest cannon fired in the United States. Situated on the south bank of the Savannah River, the stronghold saw action in the War of 1812 and the Civil War. Displays interpret the history of Savannah and the coast and include artifacts from the sunken ironclad *CSS Georgia*, as well as cannons, small arms, and tools and machinery. From December through February, the fort is open on weekends and school holidays from 9:00 A.M. to 5:00 P.M. From March through November, the fort is open Tuesday through Saturday from 9:00 A.M. to 5:00 P.M. Weapons demonstrations are given in the afternoon.

Get a different taste of the past at pre–Civil War **Fort Pulaski National Monument,** on US 80. Engineered in part by Robert E. Lee, this masterpiece of brick and masonry was thought to be invincible, but it was no match for the Union's rifled artillery. After the fort fell to the Union, it was used as a prison. Stroll through the fort or along the nature trails on the property and stop at the visitor center, which contains interpretive exhibits. The fort is open daily from 8:30 A.M. to 5:15 P.M. in the winter and from 8:30 A.M. to 6:45 P.M. in the summer. It is closed Christmas Day and New Year's Day. To learn more, call (912) 786–5787.

Several of Savannah's nineteenth-century homes are open for historical tours.

Any girl who has ever been associated with the Girl Scout movement will be intrigued by a visit to the **Juliette Gordon Low Birthplace** at 142 Bull Street. Childhood home of Juliette Gordon Low, the founder of the Girl Scouts of America, the gracious home has been restored to its 1860 to 1886 appearance and is furnished with family pieces. Young Juliette was quite artistically inclined, and many of her works are scattered throughout the house. From February through November, the house is open Monday, Tuesday, Thursday, Friday, and Saturday from 10:00 A.M. to 4:00 P.M. and Sunday from 11:00 A.M. to 4:30 P.M. In December and January the same hours apply except that the house is closed on Sundays. For more information, call (912) 233–4501.

The rich black history and culture related to Savannah and the Sea Islands are related at the **King-Tisdell Cottage of Black History Museum** (514 East Harris Street), built in 1896. View art objects, historic documents, and furnishings from the 1890s. Before you leave pick up a brochure for the **Negro Heritage Trail,** which provides three walking or driving itineraries to significant black heritage sites in Savannah. The house is open Monday through Friday from noon to 4:30 P.M. and weekends from 10:00 A.M. to 4:00 P.M. Call (912) 234–8000 for more information.

Savannah's museums delve into subjects that range from pre-history to outer space.

Fun for children of all ages, hands-on exhibits of physical and natural sciences and astronomy are on display at the **Savannah Science Museum** at 4405 Paulsen Street. Exhibits of prehistoric reptiles and amphibians native to Georgia are child-pleasers, as are planetarium shows that re-create the night skies each Sunday at 3:00 P.M. The "Mr. Wizard" science theater is presented each Saturday at 2:00 P.M. The museum is open Tuesday through Saturday from 10:00 A.M. to 5:00 P.M. and Sunday from 2:00 to 5:00 P.M. It is closed on major holidays. To learn more, call (912) 355–6705.

Those yearning to go down to the sea in ships can partially assuage their desires by making a voyage of seafaring discovery at the **Ships of the Sea Museum** at 503 East River Street. Family members can examine a large collection of models and maritime memorabilia representing 2,000 years of maritime history. Fifty intricately constructed models range in size from a few inches to more than 8 feet in length. Youngsters are spellbound by models of Viking ships, the *Mayflower*, the *SS Savannah* (the first steamship to cross the Atlantic), and the *NS Savannah* (the first nuclear-powered merchant vessel). Even more intriguing to little ones is the Ship-in-a-Bottle collection of seventy-five minuscule ships, but don't get so caught up in the model exhibits that you bypass any of the other ship memorabilia. The museum is open daily from 10:00 A.M. to 5:00 P.M., except that it is closed March 17, Thanksgiving, Christmas, and New Year's Day. For more information, call (912) 232–1511.

Active family members won't want to spend all their time indoors. Several participatory experiences beckon you into the great outdoors.

Discover a halcyon natural environment abundant with nature trails and a marsh boardwalk leading to ten different habitats that overflow with animals indigenous to coastal Georgia at the **Oatland Island Education Center** at 711 Sandtown Road. Peep into two 150-year-old log cabins on the 175-acre tract. The center is open Monday through Friday from 8:30 A.M. to 5:00 P.M. and Saturday from 11:00 A.M. to 5:00 P.M. between October and May. To learn more, call (912) 897-3773.

A perfect place for a family frolic is **Skidaway Island State Park,** Diamond Causeway on the Intracoastal Waterway, where facilities and activities include tent and trailer sites, a swimming pool, fishing, picnicking, a boat ramp, waterskiing, and nature trails. A small museum contains exhibits on island history and its flora and fauna. The park is open daily from 7:00 A.M. to 10:00 P.M. year-round, but during the school year the museum is open only on Monday and Friday. To find out more, call (912) 598-2301.

You can increase your children's knowledge of and regard for sea life by visiting the **Skidaway Maritime Science Complex** on Skidaway Island Drive and McWhorter Drive. Exhibits at this oceanographic center on the Skidaway River include a twelve-panel, 12,000-gallon aquarium, as well as coastal archaeological finds that interpret economic patterns on the coast from aboriginal times to the present. The complex is open Monday through Friday from 9:00 A.M. to 4:00 P.M. To learn more, call (912) 598-2496.

Here's a rare experience for your children. Using hydrophones on the tours led by **Spartina Trails**, the kids can eavesdrop on the underwater conversations of dolphins and other marine creatures. Other tours involve explorations of barrier islands, hiking, birdwatching, and fishing. To find out more about the programs, contact the organization, which operates from 746 Wheaton Street, at (912) 234-4621.

If your family is yearning for overnight wilderness adventure, the organization for you is **Wilderness Southeast** at 711 Sandtown Road. The unique outdoor school offers a variety of wilderness encounters (most overnight) ranging from sailing among the barrier islands and canoeing through the Okefenokee Swamp to beach hiking, photo safaris, and much more. For information, call (912) 897-5108.

Among Savannah's many festivals, one is world renowned.

Every child loves a parade. A mega-procession, the cavalcade at

Savannah's St. Patrick's Day Parade and Festival is miles and miles long and lasts for hours. Bands, floats, sequined costumes, high-stepping horses, and more march past—all in a sea of green. Sure to get the kids jumping up and down and clapping their hands in glee is the dalmatian unit. Hundreds of local residents deck their spotted dogs out in green collars, green bow ties, green hats, and other green costumes; cuddly squirming dalmatian puppies are pulled in wagons. Savannah's festival is the second-largest St. Patrick's Day celebration in the country—bigger even than that of Boston. In addition to the parade, a week of activities includes a church service, good food, arts and crafts, face painting, and much more. Call (912) 233–4804 for more information.

Take the time to drive outside Savannah to visit other important historical sites.

The kids will feel that they've gone back more than a century as you drive down the 1½-mile oak avenue that leads to the tabby ruins of a colonial estate at the **Wormsloe State Historic Site** at 7601 Skidaway Road on the Isle of Hope. In the visitor center, family members can see an audiovisual presentation about the founding of Georgia and view artifacts excavated at the site. Youngsters particularly like the colonial living history area where costumed interpreters demonstrate skills and crafts necessary to the survival of Georgia's early settlers. The site is open from 9:00 A.M. to 5:00 P.M. Tuesday through Saturday and from 2:00 to 5:30 P.M. Sunday. It is closed Mondays, Thanksgiving, and Christmas. (912) 352–2548.

Savannah is blessed with a multitude of sleeping establishments. In addition to the presence of many large chain hotels in every price range, the city has wisely allowed the use of many of its historic warehouses and commercial buildings as intimate inns and of its aristocratic old homes as cozy bed and breakfasts. The following B&Bs welcome children of any age: 17 Hundred 90 Inn, Bed & Bagel, A Bed and Breakfast, Bed and Breakfast Inn, Eliza Thompson House, Foley House, Forsyth Park Inn, Joan's on Jones, Lion's Head Inn, Magnolia Place Inn, Presidents' Quarters, Pulaski Square Inn, and St. Julian Bed and Breakfast. These B&Bs have an age restriction (generally older than twelve): 118 West, Ballastone Inn and Townhouse, Comer House, The Gastonian, and the Remshart-Brooks House. Two reservation services can help match you up with the best B&B for your family:

R.S.V.P Savannah (800–729–7787) and **Savannah Historic Inns and Guest Houses** (912–233–7666).

Close to the action along Factor's Walk, River Street, and East Bay Street, several commercial buildings have been converted to inns: the **Mulberry Inn, East Bay Inn, Old Harbour Inn,** and **River Street Inn.** Several blocks back is the regal **Planters Inn.** These are furnished with period reproductions and often have a restaurant.

Among Savannah's many outstanding restaurants are two that are particularly enjoyable for families.

Sit down to a bountiful all-you-can-eat feast of southern home cooking served family style at **Mrs. Wilkes Boarding House,** 107 Jones Street. Folks come from all over the world to eat here, so you'll probably have some very interesting table mates. Lunch is the only meal served. It's wise to get in line early (about 11:00 A.M.), because the restaurant doesn't take reservations. There's no phone and they accept no credit cards.

The children will be intrigued by the rich historic setting of the **Pirates House** at 20 East Broad Street. This authentic tavern built in 1733 serves daily lunch and dinner, with an emphasis on seafood. Brunch is served on Sunday. For more information, call (912) 233–5757.

Savor fresh seafood right off the boats at several restaurants in Thunderbolt, a shrimping village along the Intracoastal Waterway off US 80 between Savannah and the beaches of Tybee Island. Thunderbolt is a great place to let the youngsters watch working shrimp boats.

TYBEE ISLAND

Offering thrills and excitement for families, **Tybee Mountain Water Park,** #3 Fifteenth Street, features a water slide, an amusement park, and miniature golf. The water park is open daily from 10:00 A.M. to 10:00 P.M. from May to September. To learn more about the park, call (912) 786–5552.

The labyrinthine tunnels at **Fort Screven,** off US 80, are perfect for exploring by curious youngsters. Built in 1875, the fortification was manned during the Spanish-American War and both World Wars I and II. In addition to the military displays, there's a presentation about Tybee Island's resort era of the 1920s and 1930s, and an unexpected doll exhibit. The fort is open daily except Tuesday in the winter from 1:00 P.M. to 5:00 P.M.; in the summer it is open daily from 10:00 A.M. to 6:00 P.M. Call (912) 786–4077.

Get your daily exercise by climbing to the top of the 154-foot **Tybee Island Lighthouse,** located at the north end of the beach. Built in 1887, the lighthouse was one of the first public structures in Georgia. Adjacent to the light is a keeper's cottage containing a small museum with exhibits about the light. From May through September, the lighthouse and museum are open daily from 10:00 A.M. to 6:00 P.M.; the remainder of the year they are open daily from 1:00 to 5:00 P.M. For more information, call (912) 786–4077.

On a rainy day, a family visit to the **Marine Science Center** (1510 Strand at Sixteenth Avenue), an interpretive facility with exhibits and an aquarium, is both educational and entertaining. On nice days, a hit with families is the organized beach walk. The center is open daily in the summer from 9:00 A.M. to 4:00 P.M. For more information, call (912) 786–5917.

RICHMOND HILL

The past is preserved for you to see at **Fort McAllister State Historic Park,** Fort McAllister Road. A key earthwork fortification defending Savannah during the Civil War, the fortress fell to Sherman's troops in December 1864. A museum contains Civil War artifacts and today the park offers tent and trailer sites, pioneer camping, a boat dock, a boat ramp, fishing, picnicking, and nature trails. The museum is open from 9:00 A.M. to 5:00 P.M. Tuesday through Saturday and 2:00 to 5:30 P.M. on Sunday. It is closed Mondays, Thanksgiving, and Christmas. The park facilities are open daily from 7:00 A.M. to 10:00 P.M. To find out more, call (912) 727–2339.

MIDWAY

Take a peek into the past at the **Midway Museum** on US 17. Located in a raised-style cottage patterned after those typically built on the coast in the early eighteenth century, the museum contains artifacts including furniture, documents, and other memorabilia that represent the late-eighteenth and early-nineteenth centuries. Next door is the **Midway Church,** which was built in 1792. It remains a classic example of colonial New England–style architecture, having never been modernized with a heating system or electricity. The small congregation, which had worshiped in several earlier structures, produced two signers of the Declaration of Independence, two Revolutionary War generals, and a U.S. senator. From the museum, get a brochure for the self-guided tour of the Midway Cemetery, then challenge the children to find the oldest tombstone in the adjacent colonial-era burial ground and the crack in the wall that legend says has never been success-fully mended because of the ghost of a murdered slave. The museum is open Tuesday through Saturday from 9:00 A.M. to 5:00 P.M. and Sunday from 2:00 to 5:30 P.M. For more information, call (912) 884–5837.

Mention "dead town" and you're sure to pique the children's inter-est. They can learn about the former town of Sunbury and about Revolutionary War action at the **Fort Morris Historic Site** (exit 13 off I–95). Among the sights are Revolutionary War earthwork fortifications and a museum containing a cannon display, a diorama depicting the town of Sunbury, and information and artifacts concerning the Revolutionary War and the War of 1812. The site is open from 9:00 A.M. to 5:00 P.M. Tuesday through Saturday and from 2:00 to 5:30 P.M. on Sunday. It is closed Mondays, Thanksgiving, and Christmas. Call (912) 884–5999.

A wonderful place to introduce children to the lives of early coastal black residents is at **Seabrook Village** on Trade Hill Road. This African-American living history museum is dedicated to an authentic portrayal of a turn-of-the-century black community. Little people can watch cane being ground, syrup being cooked, and nets being made for shrimping. The vil-lage is open Tuesday through Saturday from 10:00 A.M. to 5:00 P.M. Call (912) 884 7008.

HINESVILLE

At **Fort Stewart's Victory Museum,** Wilson and Utility streets, the kids can linger to their heart's content over the weapons, uniforms, flags, equip-ment, vehicles, and historic photos from the Civil War to the present. Of particular interest are special collections relating to the Civil War's Merrill's Marauders, the Spanish-American War, the Philippine Insurrection, and Desert Storm. The museum is open Tuesday through Friday from noon to 4:00 P.M. and weekends from 1:00 to 5:00 P.M. except federal holidays. Call (912) 767–7885 for more information.

MCRAE

The world-record largemouth bass was caught in the **Ocmulgee River** in Telfair County in 1932. It weighed 22 pounds, 4 ounces. Needless to say, the area is renowned for its good fishing, although anglers are still trying to top that record. If your family owns a boat, access to fishing, boating, and other activities on the river is easy at six boat landings: **Telfair County Boat Landing**, US 341 bridge; **McRae's Landing**, State 117; **Burkett's Ferry**, State 117; **Staves Landing**, State 117; **Jacksonville Landing**, US 441; and **McRannie Landing**, State 117.

An excellent family-oriented resort, **Little Ocmulgee State Park,** US 441, abounds with attractions and activities for every family member. Among its other attractions, the park is the home of the eighteen-hole championship **Wallace Adams Golf Course**. In addition to the course, the golf facility also features a pro shop, cart rental, driving range, and a chipping/putting green. If the kids aren't into regular golf yet, let them try their hands at the miniature golf course. You can camp or stay in cottages or in the 30-room **Little Ocmulgee Lodge,** which also features the **Fairway Restaurant**. Other activities at the park include picnicking facilities, a boat ramp, a boat dock, waterskiing, fishing boat and canoe rental, a fishing lake, a swimming pool, tennis courts, and a nature trail. The park is open daily from 7:00 A.M. to 10:00 P.M. To learn more, call (912) 868–7474.

HAZELHURST

Anglers of all ages will find the **Altamaha River** to be a fishing paradise. The largest watershed east of the Mississippi River, the Altamaha is one of the premier largemouth bass rivers in southeast Georgia. In addition, the river is very popular for boating and waterskiing. Access to the river is provided at several boat landings. The main entrance is on US 301N.

BAXLEY

Kids will come out science fans even if they weren't when they went in after a visit to the **Edwin I. Hatch Nuclear Plant Visitor Center** on US 1. A showcase for nuclear energy, the center features animated exhibits, films, and special effects. It's open Monday through Friday from 9:00 A.M.

to 5:00 P.M. and Sunday from 1:00 to 5:00 P.M. Call (912) 367–3668.

DARIEN

Darien was founded in 1736 by General Oglethorpe's Scottish Highlanders and later became a prosperous town favored by timber barons and sea captains. Today Darien is the home of a busy shrimping fleet and is known for caviar processing. A **scenic byway**, State 99 between exits 9 and 10 (paralleling I-95) crosses the 19,000-acre **Altamaha Waterfowl Wildlife Management Area** and provides open vistas of tidal marshes and numerous species of waterfowl.

An escape to the past can be your family's at **Fort King George State Historic Site** (US 17), a reconstruction of the early eighteenth-century fort and blockhouse. In the interpretive museum you'll first see a short film about the site's history and then see artifacts from the Native American, Spanish missionary, and English settler eras. Living history demonstrations are given periodically. The historic site is open from 9:00 A.M. to 5:00 P.M. Tuesday through Saturday and from 2:00 to 5:30 P.M. Sunday. It is closed Mondays, Thanksgiving, and Christmas. To learn more, call (912) 437–4770.

SAPELO ISLAND

A naturalist's and environmentalist's heaven, Sapelo Island is accessed only by ferry from Meridian and Darien. Advance reservations are required. Call the Darien Welcome Center at (912) 437–4192 for more information or schedules.

If there are scuba divers in your family, Georgia offers only one natural marine habitat— **Gray's Reef**, 17 nautical miles off Sapelo Island. If you're lucky, you'll see sponges, hard coral, gorgonions, bryozoans, tropical fish, and dolphins. Contact the Island Dive Center (800) 940–3483 for information about diving the reef.

An absorbing place for naturalists in the family is the **Sapelo Island Estuarine Research Reserve.** Tours include the **Georgia Marine Research Institute**, the exterior of the mansion formerly owned by tobacco magnate R. J. Reynolds, miles of pristine beaches, and the delicate salt marsh ecosystem. Excursions are available Wednesday and Saturday, September through May; Wednesday, Friday, and Saturday from June to August; and the last Tuesday of each month March through October. For more information, call (912) 437–4192 or 437–6684.

BRUNSWICK

"When the children ask you "Are we there yet?," you can tell them that you're there when they see the huge chipped and broken red brick chimney from the **Factory that Never Was** at exit 7 on I–95. In 1917 Glynn County was chosen as the site for a massive factory intended to produce a vital war material used in explosives. On November 11, 1918, just thirty days from the scheduled completion of the factory, the war ended. All work on the structure immediately halted, never to be resumed. Most of the original factory buildings were demolished and now the chimney is the sole survivor. It's always accessible. There's no phone.

Step out of the frenetic modern world and into the serenity of nature by strolling along the **Earth Day Nature Trail** at One Conservation Way off US 17. The trail winds across salt marshes, tidal ponds, and coastal hammock high ground. From an observation deck and tower youngsters can scrutinize the osprey/eagle nesting platform. The trail is accessible daily from 7:00 A.M. to 6:00 P.M. For more information, call (912) 264–7218.

Focus on early coastal history at **Hofwyl-Broadfield Plantation State Historic Site** (5556 US 17), an antebellum rice plantation. The house, circa 1851, is filled with original furnishings and is surrounded by magnificent live oaks. Don't miss the orientation film and the artifacts contained in the museum. The site is open from 9:00 A.M. to 5:00 P.M. Tuesday through Saturday and 2:00 P.M. to 5:30 P.M. on Sunday. It is closed Mondays, Thanksgiving, and Christmas. Call (912) 264–7333 to learn more.

Little girls and boys and even parents are dazzled by the 3,000 dolls and antique toys displayed at the **Mary Miller Doll Museum** at 1523 Glynn Avenue. One of the largest museums of its type in the Southeast, it is open Monday through Saturday from 11:00 A.M. to 5:00 P.M. Call (912) 267–7569.

Brunswick is one of the shrimping capitals of the world, so don't leave town without strolling along the shrimp docks, at Bay Street between Gloucester and Prince streets, to see working shrimp boats. You'll also learn much about the coast and the barrier islands at the **Welcome Centers for Brunswick and the Golden Isles.** One is on I–95 southbound between exits 8 and 9 (912–264–5337); the other is on US 17 at the St. Simons Causeway (912–264–0202). Children will want to make a close-up examination of a large model of a **Liberty Ship** on the lawn of the St. Simons Causeway location. The model commemorates Brunswick's contribution to World War II. During the war the Brunswick Shipyard built ninety-nine of the 447-foot-long cargo vessels.

ST. SIMONS ISLAND

St. Simons has a long and colorful history. Millions of readers have fallen under the island's spell by reading the trilogy of historical novels by Eugenia Price: *Lighthouse, New Moon Rising,* and *Beloved Invader.* If you haven't read them, you should do so—before or after visiting the island. St. Simons was first inhabited by Guale Indians (pronounced "wally"), then French explorers landed in the sixteenth century, followed by Spanish Jesuit and later Franciscan missionaries, who attempted unsuccessfully to convert the Indians. In 1736, the English established the town of Frederica and built a fort on the banks of the river. Among the settlers were John and Charles Wesley, Anglican missionaries who sowed the seeds of Methodism here before they returned to England to found the Methodist Church. The abundance of sturdy live oaks on the island resulted in a dynamic timber industry, and great antebellum plantations grew the world-famous Sea Island cotton. Aaron Burr spent a month at Hampton Plantation following the duel in which he killed Alexander Hamilton. Just prior to the Civil War, English actress Fanny Kemble lived at Hampton Plantation, after which she wrote the *Journal of a Residence on a Georgia Plantation*—an exposé that was instrumental in arousing anti-slavery sentiment in the North and in England. Retreat Plantation was visited by John James Audubon.

Introduce the children to the history of the island by stopping at a monument that marks the **Bloody Marsh Battle Site,** Demere Road, where a small force of British troops defeated the Spanish coming from Florida in 1742.

Slaves once lived in the primitive cabins on Hamilton Plantation, now **Epworth-by-the-Sea** (100 Arthur Drive), a Methodist center on the Intracoastal Waterway. Today your children can trace their footsteps by inspecting the cabins. In addition, you can trace the history of Methodism at the center's museum. Even if your family is not attending a retreat or conference at the center, you can get inexpensive accommodations here. For information, call (912) 638–8688.

A visit to **Fort Frederica National Monument** on Frederica Road provides youngsters with an excellent history lesson. The site encompasses the ruins of the fort, the tabby powder magazine, and excavations of the village of Frederica—all built by General Oglethorpe in 1736. A visitor center/museum offers a film, artifacts, and dioramas that give insight into the lives of Native Americans, explorers, and early settlers. The site is open daily from 9:00 A.M. to 6:00 P.M. during the summer and from 9:00 A.M. to 5:00 P.M. the remainder of the year. It is closed only on Christmas Day. Call (912) 638–3639.

Several locations on St. Simons provide access to family activities at the beach or on the Intracoastal Waterway. The **Coast Guard Station,** East Beach, provides beach access and restrooms. Drive to **Gascoigne Bluff,** where timbers from strong live oaks were cut for the construction of the famous ship *Constitution*, fondly known as "Old Ironsides." Family fun, including fishing and water sports, begins at the marina and boat launch there; a concession stand satisfies hunger and thirst cravings. You'll find restaurants, shops, fuel and charter services, jet skis, and parasailing at the **Golden Isles Marina** on St. Simons Causeway (912–634–1128). **Gould's Inlet** on Bruce Drive features a beach, boardwalk, and fishing pier. **Massengale Park** on Ocean Boulevard features picnicking facilities, a beach, swimming, and showers. The island's premier park is **Neptune Park** at St. Simons Village (912–638–9014). It provides picnicking facilities, a fishing pier, crabbing, miniature golf, live theater in the fall and spring, a large swimming pool, the town library, and a visitor center.

For the truly adventurous family, **Kayak Nature Tours,** which operates out of Ocean Motion at 1300 Ocean Boulevard, conducts two-hour guided tours of the coast, marsh creeks, and secluded beaches—all easily accessible by stable touring kayaks. To learn more, call (912) 638–5225.

A resort that caters to families, the palatial beachfront **King & Prince Beach Resort** (Arnold Road at Downing Street) offers tennis, swimming, and golf at the Hampton Club Golf Course at Hampton Plantation. For information, call (912) 638–3631 or (800) 342–0212.

By climbing the 129 steps to the top of the 1872 lighthouse at the **Lighthouse and Coastal Museum** at 101 Twelfth Street, your youngsters can experience the light keeper's daily chore of illuminating the beacon. Don't forget to take the camera, because from the balcony around the light you can get some wonderful pictures of St. Simons Village. Back on ground level, examine the displays about the history of lighthouses and St. Simons Island in the museum of coastal history located in the keeper's cottage. The lighthouse and museum are open from 10:00 A.M. to 5:00 P.M. Tuesday through Saturday and from 1:30 to 5:00 P.M. on Sunday. Call (912) 638–4666.

During a **Salt Marsh Nature Tour** provided by Inland Charter Boat Service (North First Street) young people are kept busy studying nature. Operated by Frank and Janet Mead, the 1½-hour pontoon boat ride glides through tidal creeks and salt marsh while docents accredited by the UGA Marine Extension Service point out the animals, fish, birds, and flora. Optional tours include birdwatching and shelling excursions to Pelican Spit. For information on day, evening, and sunset tours, call (912) 638–3611, ext 5202.

To acquaint the family with the significant sites on St. Simons, there's hardly a better way than to board a **St. Simons Trolley** for a tour. The trolley departs from the St. Simons Village area Tuesday through Saturday at 11:00 A.M., 1:00 P.M., and 3:00 P.M. during the summer months. During the winter there is only one tour, at 1:00 P.M. For more information, call (912) 638–8954.

SEA ISLAND

Part of the Old Spanish Main, Sea Island—originally called Long Island— is among the most historic territories in America. It has been four centuries since European explorers set foot on these shores. First the French and then the Spanish attempted to colonize the area before the English ultimately succeeded. In 1926 Howard E. Coffin, one of the founders of the Hudson Motor Car Company, bought Long Island and changed its name. Two years later he built **The Cloister Hotel** (100 First Street), one of the world's great resorts.

Beach time is a favorite activity at Cloister's Sea Island Summer Camp.

Opened in 1928, the magnificent resort is Georgia's only Mobil five-star and AAA five-diamond property. Mediterranean red-tile-roof-topped architecture is surrounded by colorful gardens and lush foliage, and the luxurious accommodations range from rooms and suites in the main inn to beachfront units and cottages. Adding to the elegant resort's extraordinary appeal are five miles of sparkling beaches, a beach club, golf courses, an eighteen-hole putting green, a nine-hole pitch-and-putt course, eighteen tennis courts, a health spa, croquet courts, trap and skeet shooting, two pools, horseback riding, fishing, boating, swimming, and diving. *Golf* and *Tennis* magazines rate the facilities at the Cloister as among the best places in the country to enjoy these sports. A staff of pros offers instruction at reasonable fees. A mustn't-miss activity for the whole family is the jeep train safari around the island.

Children in the same room with their parents stay free except for a meal charge based on age. There is no charge for golf greens fees and afternoon tennis for those guests younger than nineteen. While the children frolic at their own pursuits, parents can indulge in ultimate pampering at the Cloister's **Sea Island Beach Club Spa and Salon.** Among the gratifying services offered at the spa are manicures, soothing facials, therapeutic massages, body treatments, Swiss showers, hydrotherapy, reflexology, makeup sessions, spa cuisine, and exercise sessions.

Every day except Sunday during the Cloister's **Summer Family Festival,** children can cavort at the **Sea Island Summer Camp,** which lasts from the week after the Fourth of July through Labor Day. Included in the daily rate, the structured schedule has energetic activities for all tastes and ages. Cloister Cubs are ages three and four, Sea Island Sandpipers are five through eight, and the Gazebo Gang is designed for ages nine through eleven. Teen activities are less structured but include sports, parties, and dances. Although children are welcome at any of the dining options, including the formal Main Dining Room, many prefer to participate in the Children's Dinner and Playtime from 6:00 to 9:00 P.M. Tuesday through Friday. Junior Tennis Clinics for ages six through twelve, Junior Golf Clinics for ages seven through sixteen, and a few other special activities incur a small extra charge. During the Summer Family Festival, meals are included without charge for children younger than nineteen sharing the same room with their parents. Similar programs are available during holiday periods and Spring Break. For more information or reservations, call (912) 638–3611 or (800) SEA–ISLAnd.

For added fun, take the kids on a **Salt Marsh Boat Ride** from the Sea Island Fishign Dock. Captain Jim and Jeanne Pleasants conduct wildlife observation rides in conjunction with narrated tours of the salt marsh, as well as shelling and nature tours. Call (912) 638–3611, extension 5202 or (912) 638–9354.

If you or your children have ever yearned to ride horseback on the beach, **Sea Island Stables** at Sea Island and Frederica roads offers rides along the marsh or to a private beach. During the summer you can take part in one of the most exciting and memorable treats of all time by riding bareback into the sea and swimming with your horse. The stable, which provides both English and western saddles, also offers picnics on Tuesday and Saturday. A great site for a birthday party, the stable yard is filled with freely wandering farm animals sure to delight the younger children. The stables are open every day except Christmas morning. Call (912) 638–1032.

LITTLE ST. SIMONS ISLAND

A place to make wonderful memories for youngsters, parents, and even grandparents is Little St. Simons Island. Although restricted to children older than six, the privately owned island is a family adventure paradise. Accessible only by a twice-daily ferry, Little St. Simons has been owned for more than 100 years by the Berolzheimer family, who open it up to visitors several times a year. The 10,000-acre island caters to only twenty-four guests at time in accommodations that range from a turn-of-the-century lodge to several more modern cottages built in the 1980s. Truly a place to get away from it all, Little St. Simons has no radio, TV, or newspapers, and only one phone. But you won't even think about them. In addition to enjoying the 7 miles of unspoiled beaches, activities include hiking, horseback riding, fishing, canoeing, kayaking, and nature study. In fact, the resort has on-staff naturalists to take you on turtle hunts and deer counts or to introduce you to freely roaming deer, soaring eagles, alligators, armadillos, and myriad species of birds. At this extremely casual getaway, all you need to bring are your camera, your bathing suit, and a big appetite.

Meals and activities are included in the price. For more information or reservations, call (912) 638–7472.

Because the Little St. Simons resort staff wants its visitors to experience some of the same activities as have generations of the Berolzheimer family who grew up spending significant periods of time on the island, they have developed the **Summer Fun for Families** program. Using the island as a natural classroom to encourage exploration, the program includes scavenger hunts, lessons in map and compass reading, role-playing in the Food Chain Game, safaris, fishing with seine and cast nets, fish printing—an arts and crafts activity—and much more. To learn more about the program, call (912) 638–7472.

WAYCROSS

Waycross received its name because it held a strategic position where stagecoach roads and pioneer trails crossed. In addition, it is one of the gateways to the **Okefenokee Swamp** (see also Fargo on page 125 and Folkston on page 126), labeled by Native Americans as the "Land of the Trembling Earth."

Providing a rare glimpse into a late-1800s swamper's lifestyle, **Obediah's Okefenok** at 500 Obediah Trail off Swamp Road honors Obediah Barber, who was known as the "King of the Okefenokee." Children are fascinated by the story of the 6-foot, 6-inch swamper who was also known as the "Southeast Paul Bunyan." They love the spine-tingling legend of his encounter with a huge black bear—a confrontation in which Obediah emerged the victor. In the early 1800s Obediah was one of the first white settlers to live on the northern frontier of the Okefenokee Swamp. As a youngster he assisted state surveyors in determining the true boundary line between the state of Georgia and the territory of Florida. As an adult he married three times, fathered twenty children, and made his living as a hunter, trapper, and cattle farmer. During the Civil War Odediah provided beef to the Confederacy. Your children can let their imaginations run free while scampering through the homestead, which combines Obediah's historic log home with a dozen historic farm buildings and more than fifty exhibits of artifacts from the period, including a turpentine shed and a moonshine still. In addition, children love the petting zoo and the boardwalks and trails for wildlife observation. Scheduled events and living history demonstrations portray the life of a swamper as well as Native American culture. Visit Obediah's Okefenok Monday through Saturday from 10:00 A.M. to 5:00 P.M. and Sunday from 2:00 to 4:00 P.M. The complex is closed Christmas, New Year's Day, Easter, and Thanksgiving. To find out more, call (912) 287–0090.

The children can learn more about the heritage and lives of the people who settled in the vicinity of the Okefenokee Swamp at the **Okefenokee Heritage Center** on North Augusta Avenue. Primary among the exhibits that excite a child's imagination are a 1912 Baldwin steam locomotive, a tender, and additional rail cars on which they can clamber aboard. The collection of carriages and vintage cars is sure to appeal to youngsters of all ages, but there's even more—a 1900s print shop, the General Thomas Hilliard house, and an 1840s farmhouse with typical outbuildings. Classes, workshops, lectures, films, and tours are scheduled here throughout the year. The center is open Tuesday through Saturday from 10:00 A.M. to 5:00 P.M. and Sunday from 2:00 to 4:00 P.M. It is closed Mondays and major holidays. Call (912) 285–4260 to learn more.

Where else can children walk inside a giant Loblolly pine, see a mummified dog in a tree, or listen to a talking tree than at **Southern Forest World** at 1440 North Augusta Avenue? Members of your family can increase their knowledge of the timbering industry by visiting this educational exhibit center where the story of forestry in the thirteen southern states is told. Youngsters can learn about forest industries, study naval stores operations of yesterday and today, and gain an understanding of the managed forest concept. In addition to trees they can climb, kids can see a collection of logging tools, climb the fire tower to observe the area, and explore the nature trails. The interpretive center is open daily from 9:00 A.M. to 5:30 P.M. Call (912) 285–4056 for more information.

A visit to the **Okefenokee Swamp Park** on US 1/23S will intrigue the entire family. The highlight of any visit is a guided boat tour down the dark, reflective, lily-decked waters of the mysterious swamp, but children can also be kept totally engrossed for hours at the serpentarium, the wildlife observatory, the Swamp Creation Center with the Living Swamp display, an exhibit about the Wildes Family Massacre, and the swamp homestead. Check for the schedule of periodic interpretive lectures and wildlife shows held through the year. Canoe rentals are available for the active family. The park is open from 9:00 A.M. to 6:30 P.M. between June and August and from 9:00 A.M. to 5:30 P.M. the remainder of the year. For more information, call (912) 283–0583 or 285–4260.

DOUGLAS

Observe the process of grain being ground right before your eyes at **Lott's Grist Mill** at 5772 Mora Road in Willacoochee. In addition to observing meal being ground at the working gristmill, children can get involved in hands-on activities such as cleaning, grinding, and bagging the corn. After that, they can get acquainted with the farm animals. The mill is open Monday through Saturday from 9:00 A.M. to 5:00 P.M. Call (912) 384–6858.

FITZGERALD

Satisfy your curiosity about the Civil War at the **Blue-Gray Museum** in the Municipal Building/Old Depot on Johnston Street, where both Confederate and Union relics from the Civil War are on display. The museum is open from April through September, Monday through Friday from 2:00 to 5:00 P.M. Call (912) 423–5375.

FARGO

Fargo is one of the gateways to the greatest family adventure you can imagine. Called "America's greatest natural botanical garden," the **Okefenokee Swamp** is one of Mother Nature's most bizarre creations. The 950-square mile depression is the largest swamp in the country and supports a profusion of vegetation, fish, bird, and animal life. A perfect place for a day trip, the swamp also offers challenging overnight canoeing/camping experiences.

One of the entrances to the Okefenokee National Wildlife Refuge is **Stephen C. Foster State Park** on State 177. The park provides boat tours, boat rentals, fishing, canoeing, camping, cottages, a museum, and a camp store. Hours vary seasonally, so it's a good idea to call ahead. To learn more or to make reservations, call (912) 637–5274.

FOLKSTON

Folkston is another of the gateways to the Okefenokee Swamp. A truly fantastic place for families to spend a day is at the **Okefenokee National Wildlife Refuge** on State 121/123, where the orientation center offers films about the swamp and exhibits about its animal life. Drive or bicycle to the **Chesser Island Homestead**, a restored swamp dwelling which demonstrates to youngsters the self-sufficiency that was necessary for pioneer swamp families to survive. Among the hiking trails active families can experience are the **Canal Diggers Trail**, the **Peckerwood Trail**, and the **Deer Stand Trail**. In addition, the park features a 4,000-foot boardwalk and a 50-foot observation tower from which you can get good views of the swamp. From March through mid-September the refuge is open daily from 7:00 A.M. to 7:00 P.M.; the interpretive center is open from 9:00 A.M. to 4:00 P.M.. The remainder of the year the refuge is open daily except Christmas from 8:00 A.M. to 6:00 P.M., and the interpretive center is open from 10:00 A.M. to 4:00 P.M. To learn more about the refuge, call (912) 496–7836. At the same location, the **Suwanee Canal Recreation Area** offers guided boat tours, boat and canoe rentals, and a refreshment center. From March through mid-September the concessionaire is open from 7:00 A.M. to 7:30 P.M.; the remainder of the year it is open from 8:00 A.M. to 6:00 P.M. To find out more, call (912) 496–7156 or (800) SWAMP 96.

JEKYLL ISLAND

From 1886 to 1942, Jekyll Island was the private retreat of 100 wealthy families who came primarily in the winter to hunt. This was no rustic hunting camp, however. The millionaires built a magnificent Victorian club/hotel and individual "cottages" that we'd consider mansions. For added amusement, they built a nine-hole golf course and outdoor and indoor tennis courts. After World War II, the island was abandoned by the rich and famous and was eventually purchased by the state of Georgia, which regulates its development. Now, in addition to restoration of the millionaire's district, Jekyll Island offers 10 miles of beach, hotel/motel properties in every price range, and numerous family-oriented recreational opportunities.

Let your children see what the extravagant lifestyle of the millionaires was like by touring the **Jekyll Island Club National Landmark Historic**

District. Traveling through the tree-shaded district by trolley, you will tour the insides of several of the restored mansion-size "cottages," admiring their opulent period furnishings and decorative arts as well as historical photographs of turn-of-the-century life on the island. From the Museum Orientation Center located in the Old Stables on Stable Road, tours depart on the hour from 10:00 A.M. until 3:00 P.M. daily except Christmas Day and New Year's Day. To find out more, call (912) 635–2119.

Family members can actually experience a small part of the millionaire's lifestyle by staying at the **Radisson Jekyll Island Club Hotel** (371 Riverview Drive) a restored turn-of-the-century National Historic Landmark. The four-star, four-diamond property combines Victorian opulence with all the modern amenities to offer spacious, high-ceilinged guest rooms and suites furnished with faithfully reproduced nineteenth-century pieces. Most accommodations sport a decorative fireplace and some boast whirlpool baths. In addition, the resort hotel features casual and fine dining, a croquet court, bicycle rentals, a private beach club, a heated swimming pool, and a putting green.

From early June through mid-August, the hotel offers a children's program called **Club Juniors.** The program consists of a half-day or all-day schedule of events for children five through twelve years of age. Activities include bicycle safaris, beach fun, crabbing, arts and crafts, tennis, lawn sports, swimming, kite flying, and excursions to both the Summer Waves water park and Jekyll Island's miniature golf course. Lunch is included with the full-day program and can be provided at an extra charge for half-day participants. Friday culminates with "That's Entertainment," a special series with visits from Okefenokee Joe and the Snakes, magicians, puppeteers, storytellers, and more. Non-guests of the hotel can also participate in Club Juniors for a higher fee. Rather than paying for the children's program separately, you can book the **Summer Family Adventure Package** for three, four, or five nights. The package, which is available Sunday through Thursday nights, includes accommodations, complimentary tennis, and the children's program, excluding meals and special events. For hotel information or reservations, call (912) 635–2600. For more information about Club Juniors, call (912) 635–2600.

Recreation on Jekyll Island is varied and family-oriented. Because development has been strictly limited, the beaches are uncrowded and the streets are quiet. An extensive system of Bicycle and Jogging Trails includes 20 miles of paved paths through the historic district as well as past woodlands, marshes, and along the beach. Bike rentals are available at the miniature golf course, as well as at several hotels, the campground, and the Jekyll Island Club Hotel. For more information about the bike and jogging trails, call the welcome center at (912) 635–3636.

Anglers have numerous choices for casting their lines into the water. One is to fish from the **Fishing Pier** on North Riverview Road at the Clam Creek Picnic Area. To learn more, call (912) 635–3636 or (800) 841–6586. At the **Jekyll Harbor Marina** (1 Harbor Road) you'll find a complete facility with dry storage, dockage, charters, rentals, a café, and a pool and spa for marina guests. For more information about the marina, call (912) 635–3636. The **Jekyll Island Historic Marina** (#1 Pier Road off North Riverview Drive) provides dockage, deep-sea fishing charters, dinner or sunset/dolphin watch sightseeing cruises, bait and tackle, jetski and boat rentals, fishing equipment, and bike rentals. Call (912) 635–2891 for more information.

Duffers can choose from among sixty-three holes of golf on Jekyll Island: nine holes at the historic **Oceanside Course** constructed by the millionaires in 1898 and eighteen holes each at the **Oleander, Pine Lakes**, and **Indian Mounds** courses. For more information about the courses or to set up tee times, contact the golf center on Capt. Wylly Road at (912) 635–2368.

Less serious golfers in your family might prefer to try their luck at the **Miniature Golf Course** on Beachview Drive, where two lighted eighteen-hole courses are filled with animals and other obstacles. The course is open daily from 9:00 A.M. to 10:00 P.M. during the summer and from 9:00 A.M. to 5:00 P.M. fall through winter. To find out more, call (912) 635–2648.

Tennis has been important on Jekyll Island for more than 100 years. The restored **J. P. Morgan Tennis Court** at 371 Riverview Drive sports thirteen courts. One is indoors, and five are lighted. There's also a center court with grandstands. Call (912) 635–2600 for more information. The **Jekyll Island Tennis Center** on Capt. Wylly Road is an all-clay thirteen-court facility rated by *Tennis Magazine* as among its Top 25. The tennis center is open daily from 9:00 A.M. to 6:00 P.M. To learn more, call (912) 635–3154.

On a hot summer day your family will enjoy a splash at **Summer**

Waves on South Riverview Drive. For all-day fun for one price, the eleven-acre water park features several water slides, a wave pool, an endless river, a children's pool, a McDonald's, and a gift shop. From Memorial Day to Labor Day, the water park is open Sunday through Friday from 10:00 A.M. to 6:00 P.M. and Saturday from 10:00 A.M. to 8:00 P.M. To learn more, call (912) 635–2074 or (800) 841–6586.

A completely different type of family activity is yours at the **Water Ski Park** on South Riverview Drive. This innovative concept allows you to water ski without a boat. Great for all skill levels of water skiers, a system of cables pulls you around the small lake. Multiple skiers can be towed simultaneously, and you can try your hand at knee boards, trick skis, slalom skis, or even barefoot skiing. Hourly rates or daily passes are available during the park's spring-through-summer season. Between Memorial Day and Labor Day, the park is open daily from 10:00 A.M. to 7:00 P.M. From April 1 through Memorial Day and from Labor Day through October 1, the park is open only on weekends. Call (912) 635–3080 for more information.

If your family loves camping and having fun in the outdoors, you may

Enjoy a lazy ride in the sun at Summer Waves on Jekyll Island.

prefer to stay at the **Jekyll Island Campground** on North Beachview Drive. An eighteen-acre site with 200 campsites, camp store, laundry, and bike rentals, the campground is located one mile from the beach. To find out more or to reserve a space, call (912) 635–3021.

ST. MARYS

St. Marys is a quaint river village with several historic attractions that make a pleasant destination on their own. The town, however, is best known as the point of access for the Cumberland Island National Seashore (see page 131).

Don't leave St. Marys without introducing the little ones to the **Braille Trail.** Thirty-eight sites in the historic district are marked with raised letters and braille symbols for sight-impaired visitors. To find out more about the trail, call (912) 882–6200.

Everyone in the family can have fun at **Crooked River State Park** at 3092 Spur 40. Located in a beautiful coastal setting on the south bank of the Crooked River, the park offers cabins, campsites, picnicking facilities, fishing, a boat ramp and dock, and nature trails. Swimming is available in the pool from Memorial Day through Labor Day except on Monday. The park is open daily from 7:00 A.M. to 10:00 P.M. year-round. Call (912) 882–5256 to get more information.

If the family will be catching an early morning ferry to Cumberland Island, spend the previous night in one of St. Marys's historic hotels: the **Historic Spencer House Inn**, at Osborne and Bryant streets (912–882–1872), or the **Riverview Hotel** at 105 Osborne Street (912–882–3242).

CUMBERLAND ISLAND
NATIONAL SEASHORE

Accessible only via the passenger ferry *Cumberland Queen* from the downtown St. Marys waterfront, Cumberland Island is an almost untouched paradise where you can see wild horses, deer, and armadillo, or go backpacking, camping, swimming on 20 miles of pristine beach, salt water fishing, or shelling. At the turn of the twentieth century, the entire island was owned by the wealthy Carnegie family, who built several mansions there. In 1971 they donated the island to the United States for use as a national seashore. Only 300 day trippers and campers are allowed on the island daily, and, other than the few used by National Park Service, vehicles are not allowed on the island. A visit here is a walking experience. Among the sites you can see are a small museum in the **Ice House** with exhibits depicting the island's history, and the ruins of **Dungeness** and **Stafford** mansions. Occasionally tours are offered to the **Plum Orchard** mansion, which is in excellent condition. There are no stores on Cumberland Island; you must pack in *everything* you need and pack out your trash. Reservations for the ferry and campground are required. Call (912) 882–4335 for more information or reservations.

If your idea of a good time doesn't include sleeping on the ground, families with children older than six can find one luxurious accommodation on Cumberland Island. **Greyfield Inn** was once the private residence of the Carnegie family and is still owned and operated by family members. Located on 1,300 acres within easy walking distance of the beach, the inn is furnished as it was in 1901. Although the inn isn't air conditioned, guest rooms do sport ceiling fans and are cooled by the constant sea breezes. Most of the eleven rooms share a bath. The expansive front porch is filled with rockers and huge swings—perfect for curling up in with a good book. Three gourmet meals daily are included in the nightly rate. Guests at the Greyfield Inn don't have to walk everywhere as do other visitors to Cumberland Island. Rental bicycles are available. Access to the inn is only by private ferry from Fernandina Beach, Florida. Get in touch with the inn by calling (904) 261–6408 or by writing to the inn at 8 North Second Street, Fernandina Beach, Florida 32035 0900.

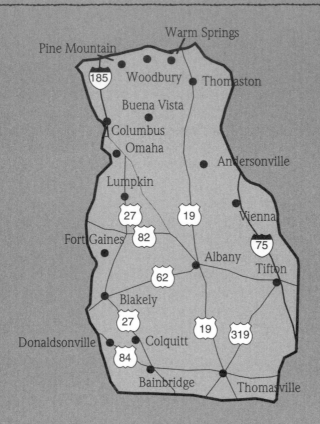

Warm Springs

Pine Mountain

185

Woodbury

Thomaston

Buena Vista

Columbus

Omaha

Andersonville

Lumpkin

27

19

Vienna

82

Fort Gaines

75

Albany

Tifton

62

Blakely

27

19

319

Donaldsonville

Colquitt

84

Bainbridge

Thomasville

Southwest Georgia

SOUTHWEST GEORGIA

eorgia's "Other Coast," the southwestern corner of the state lies along the Chattahoochee River and borders both Alabama and the Florida panhandle. This section of Georgia contains three state-designated tourism regions: the Chattahoochee Trace, the Plantation Trace, and the Presidential Pathways. The first tourism region in the country that includes two states, the Chattahoochee Trace encompasses attractions on both the Georgia and Alabama sides of the river. In the last century, the Plantation Trace contained vast numbers of plantations and attracted wealthy northerners who wintered in the mild region. Today the Plantation Trace still contains the largest concentration of working plantations in America and is being rediscovered by tourists. Franklin D. Roosevelt had a home in southwest Georgia and Jimmy Carter still lives there, hence the name Presidential Pathways. Although this region is primarily characterized by little towns, it does contain several small but vibrant cities, such as Albany, Columbus, Tifton, and Thomasville. The area contains a world-class garden, Georgia's Grand Canyon, two living history villages, several covered bridges, white-water rapids, numerous significant lakes, and ancient Indian mounds. You family's exploration of the southwestern corner of the state will be well-rewarded with historical sites, recreational opportunities, and modern, state-of-the-art attractions.

WOODBURY

Georgia is fortunate to have more than a dozen covered bridges, quaint remnants of a simpler time. Built using the Town Lattice design during the 1840s by famed black bridge builder Horace King, the 116-foot-long **Big Red Oak Creek Bridge** on State 85 4 miles north of the city is the longest wooden bridge in Georgia.

PINE MOUNTAIN

Callaway Gardens and Resort on US 27 is a place where precious family memories are made. In fact, the gardens and resort were recently voted the "best day trip from Atlanta" by readers of *Atlanta Magazine*. Cason Callaway's personal garden and experimental reclamation projects eventually developed into the fabulous 2,500-acre gardens, where gorgeous floral arrays, deep woodlands, and crystal-clear lakes serve as a backdrop for both educational and recreational pursuits. Among the spellbinding attractions in the gardens proper are one of the largest collections of azaleas in the country—including the rare orange plumleaf or prunifolia, which grows only within a 100-mile radius; 450 species of holly; the **John A. Sibley Horticultural Center**—a five-acre indoor/outdoor greenhouse; **Mr. Cason's Vegetable Garden**—the southern set for the PBS series *The Victory Garden*; the **Ida Cason Callaway Memorial Chapel**; and the **Cecil B. Day Butterfly Center,** where more than 1,000 "jewels of the air" from three continents dazzle visitors to the nation's largest glass-enclosed free-flight butterfly conservatory. Challenge the children to find different species and tell them that if they stand very still, a brilliant-hued butterfly may light on them. Cuisine at Callaway Gardens is legendary. Many of the fruits and vegetables used at the restaurants or in the prepared food items that are sold at the resort's various outlets come from the complex's own gardens. Overlooking the golf course and lake within the gardens, the Veranda restaurant serves exquisite Italian cuisine for dinner and the Gardens restaurant offers a variety of healthful luncheon choices. The activity calendar at the gardens is loaded each year with numerous classes, workshops, and special events, such as Autumn Adventures, the Steeplechase at Callaway, and Fantasy in Lights (see below). The hours that the gardens are open vary with the season, but a good rule of thumb is daylight to dusk. To learn more, call (800) CALLAWAY.

For a family vacation not soon forgotten, the family-oriented

Callaway Gardens Resort features a hotel, two-bedroom family cottages, and luxurious two-, three-, or four-bedroom villas. Perfect for family get-aways, each cottage or villa features a fully equipped kitchen, a living/dining area with a fireplace, a deck, and a screened-in porch. No matter what their age, every single family member will find a myriad of appropriate activities at the resort. Recreational amenities include sixty-three holes of championship golf, a tennis complex, fishing lakes, hiking trails, a fitness trail, boat and bike rentals, and a 7½ mile bike trail. Among the four golf courses, the Mountain View course is ranked among the top American courses by both *Golf Digest* and *GOLF* magazines. The tennis center features clay and hard courts as well as racquetball courts and a pro shop. You can take flycasting lessons from a pro at the flyfishing center, then try your luck from the banks of the lake or from a boat. On and around Robin Lake, you'll find a large beach, the *Robin E. Lee* riverboat, pedal boat rentals, and a miniature golf course, as well as a miniature train that carries visitors through heavy woods and around the lake. The highlight of the summer season is the residency of the Florida State University "Flying High" Circus, which gives eight totally different performances each week. Among the legendary dining outlets on the resort side are the inn's coat-and-tie Georgia Room and its Plantation Room, the Country Kitchen at the Callaway Gardens Country Store, the Flower Mill sandwich shop and ice cream parlor, and Champions at the golf course. In addition, there are concession stands at the beach. For more information about the resort or for reservations, call (800) CALLAWAY.

Guaranteed to create lifelong family memories, the **Summer Family Adventure program** consists of week-long sessions of all-day, everyday activities for all ages. Central to the program is the Florida State University "Flying High" Circus. In addition to the entertainment provided by the performers, the FSU students also serve as counselors for special structured activities for youngsters aged seven through teenage. In addition, child care centers are set up for infants and toddlers younger than three and for children three through six, who participate in a wide range of activities. Children seven and older are eligible to participate in the circus program, learning simple magic tricks and circus acts such as juggling, tightrope walking, tumbling, and swinging on the trapeze. Children who come back year after year progress in the difficulty of circus tricks they can perform and may actually develop into adept performers. Children who participate in the Summer Family Adventure program also take part in swimming, arts and crafts, and rides on the *Robin E. Lee* and the miniature train. Depending on their age group, older youngsters may also participate in competitive games, miniature golf, boating, dancing, ecology talks, and much more. A game room is set aside just for teens, who have their own set of activities, including hayrides, dances, and a karaoke night. Meanwhile parents can play tennis or golf, participate in arts and crafts, or just relax. Families can also participate together in such activities as beach volleyball, campfires, scavenger hunts, bike hikes, trail walks, beach bingo, storytelling, nature Olympics, and birdwatching basics. The week culminates in a recognition and awards ceremony. Families are usually accommodated in the cottages or villas, where they have access to a separate swimming pool and laundry facilities. To find out more about the summer activity program, call (800) CALLAWAY.

Callaway Garden's Christmas extravaganza is **Fantasy in Lights**, which runs from Thanksgiving week to New Year's Eve. This 5-mile ride-through audiovisual tour passes dozens of fanciful lighted scenes depicting musical Christmas cards. Youngsters think they really are in a winter wonderland, mesmerized as they are by the hundreds of thousands of white and colored lights that create gigantic toy soldiers, poinsettias, snowflakes, toys, an icicle forest, and more, but don't be fooled into thinking this is an event just for tykes—it captivates all ages. After riding through the Fantasy in Lights, the kids can visit with Santa and shop for trinkets inexpensive enough for their pocketbooks while the sounds of caroling, the smell of tangy spices, and the tastes of hot cider and hot chocolate complete the festive ambience. The admission price is per car, so the bigger your family, the more economical it is to view the fantastic light show. Tickets must be purchased in advance. To find out more about Fantasy in Lights, call (800) CALLAWAY.

What a treat the **Steeplechase at Callaway** is for the whole family. Run each November over a 2‰-mile turf oval on a beautiful 200-acre rolling course surrounded by hardwoods and pines, the handsome hunt meet provides a chance to watch stately horses maneuver around abrupt curves, up and down steep grades, and over exciting jumps. Occasional spills by both horses and riders add to the thrills and excitement. Food is an integral part of the day's activities whether you're feasting on an elegant repast in one of the sumptuous private tents, enjoying an informal tailgate picnic, or indulging in the Taste of the Chase—a sampling of dishes from different restaurants. A decorated buggy parade, junior races, and Jack Russell terrier races bring joy and delight to young ones. The resort offers a weekend package that includes admission to the races, accommodations, and other events. Call (800) CALLAWAY for the exact date and more information.

Your family will need to spend considerable time at **Franklin D. Roosevelt State Park** (2970 State 190E) in order to investigate all its amenities. Built in the 1930s by the CCC and named for the president who spent so much time in the area, the park incorporates his favorite driving route and picnic spot. Among its 10,000 acres the park features lakes, a spring-fed pool, 30 miles of hiking trails, a scenic drive, riding stables (see below), fishing, and picnicking areas. Overnight facilities include cabins, RV sites, pioneer camps, and group camps. The park is open daily from 7:00 A.M. to 10:00 P.M. To learn more, call (706) 663–4858.

Just imagine the entire family setting off on horseback for a trek up to the top of Pine Mountain, where you cook your supper over an open campfire, then sing and tell stories around the campfire before falling asleep under the stars. Well, long before *City Slickers* became a popular movie, **Roosevelt Riding Stables** on State 354 was offering overnight trail rides—complete with meals cooked from a chuck wagon—in addition to its hourly, half-day, and all-day rides. Even if the family isn't going riding, you might want to visit the stables just to see the resident buffalo or so that the children can pet or bottle feed the baby farm animals that wander unconfined around the stable yard. Bring the camera. Whether you go on a trail ride or spend time in the stable yard, you can't beat pictures of your children in close-up encounters with animals. The stables are open daily from 9:00 A.M. to 5:00 P.M. Because the daily and overnight rides are heavily booked so far in advance, reservations are strongly advised to avoid disappointment. For more information, call (706) 628–4533.

Avid hikers will want to experience all or part of the 23 miles of the blazed **Pine Mountain Trail** that runs from the Callaway Country Store

There's always something fun to do at Roosevelt Riding Stables in Pine Mountain.

on US 27 in Pine Mountain to the WJSP-TV tower on State 85W in Warm Springs. Camping facilities are available and you can get a trail map from the FDR State Park office. For information about the trail, call the state park at (706) 663-4858.

Go on a photographic safari with the kids to the **Pine Mountain Wild Animal Park** at 1300 Oak Grove Road. Zebras, camels, giraffes, and 200 or more other species of exotic creatures from every continent rove throughout the 500-acre sanctuary. Visitors can view the animals from a self guided driving tour or from a guided bus tour. The park also offers a serpentarium, an aviary, a monkey house, and authentic farm with a petting zoo, where children can actually milk a cow and bottle feed a calf. The wild animal park is open daily from 10:00 A.M. to 7:30 P.M. in the summer. It closes earlier during the winter. To find out more, call (706) 663-8744.

WARM SPRINGS

Franklin D. Roosevelt began coming to the **Village of Warm Springs** in 1924 to obtain treatments from the healing waters to relieve the pain of his polio. Eventually, in 1932—the same year he became president—Roosevelt built himself a small house here. Whenever FDR was in residence, the town became a beehive of activity, filled with the press, the Secret Service, Hollywood stars, and visiting dignitaries. When the president died at the Little White House in 1945, the town folded up and slept—almost completely forgotten—for more than forty years. Today, however, Warm Springs is revitalized as a tourist town that sports sixty-five quaint shops and restaurants.

Tour Roosevelt's **Little White House Historic Site** (State 85W), which includes the simple white frame three bedroom cottage that is the only home FDR ever owned. The house remains as it was the day the president died on April 12, 1945. You'll see the famous unfinished portrait for which the president was sitting when he became ill. Make sure to point out to the children the leash still hanging on a peg by the door. It belonged to Roosevelt's little Scottish terrier, Fala. Take the stone path up the hill to the museum. The path is lined with stones representative of a rock indigenous to each state. It's fun to see if the youngsters can find the stone from

Georgia or that of any other state in which you've lived. Once you've reached the museum, the youngsters can examine memorabilia from Roosevelt's life and presidency. The site is open from 9:00 A.M. to 5:00 P.M. every day except Thanksgiving and Christmas. For more information, call (706) 655–5870.

If you want the youngsters to get a better idea about the Roosevelt era, stay at the **Hotel Warm Springs** at 17 Broad Street. The 1907 three-story hotel has been restored to represent its 1941 appearance—the time when FDR was president and the hotel was frequented by the glitterati. The president himself would come by for a Coke from the hotel's drugstore and stay for a chat with townsfolk. Contained in the soaring lobby are the original switchboard, typewriter, and phone booth. What stories they could probably tell! Spacious, high-ceilinged guest rooms are filled with Roosevelt memorabilia, collectibles, and antiques. Some are furnished with the original oak pieces manufactured by Eleanor Roosevelt's Val-Kill Shop in Hyde Park, New York. In addition, the hotel features a restaurant, an ice cream parlor, and several gift shops. A full country breakfast is included in the nightly rate. For more information or reservations, call (800) 366–7616.

Giving little ones an idea of what's involved in raising fish to be stocked in Georgia's lakes and streams, the **Warm Springs Regional Fisheries Center** on US 27 ALT features a hatchery, a fish health center, a visitor center, and several aquarium displays. The hatchery is open daily from 7:30 A.M. to 4:00 P.M. Call (706) 655–3382.

THOMASTON

Another great place for families who love high adventure is the Flint River. Those who yearn for thrills and chills can canoe the Flint's class I, II, and III rapids from the **Flint River Outdoor Center** on State 36. Organized and unguided trips are available for excursions of one-half to four days. Reservations are required for guided trips. Other services provided by the center include a shuttle service, canoe and raft rentals, camping, and concessions. From Memorial Day to Labor Day, the center is open from 10:00 A.M. to 8:00 P.M. weekdays and 8:00 A.M. to 8:00 P.M. on weekends; the rest of the year excursions are by appointment. To learn more, call (706) 647–2633.

Sprewell Bluff, on Old Alabama Road 8 miles west of town off State

74, provides a stunning view of the Flint River gorge. The river park features hiking trails and a boat ramp as well as being a super place for a picnic. South of town 12 miles on Allen Road is the **Auchumpkee Covered Bridge,** built in 1893 in the Town Lattice design. Both sites are always accessible.

COLUMBUS

The **Columbus Museum** (1251 Wynnton Road) is the second-largest museum in Georgia and has an outstanding art collection sure to please any adult or budding art lover. Younger family members, however, will probably be most interested in the Chattahoochee Legacy, a regional history gallery that uses a film of the same name as well as life-size period settings to relate the story of the Chattahoochee River Valley region. In addition, Transformations is a hands-on gallery for children where exhibits and activities are designed to arouse their curiosity and excite their imaginations. The museum is open Tuesday through Saturday from 10:00 A.M. to 5:00 P.M. and Sunday from 1:00 to 5:00 P.M. Call (706) 649–0713 for more information.

Baseball fans who don't have easy access to a major league team or who find watching the big teams too impersonal might enjoy watching the **Columbus Redstixx** baseball team, the minor league farm team of the Cleveland Indians. The Redstixx play at Golden Park, Lumpkin Boulevard, from April thorugh August. Golden Park will be the center of world attention during the 1996 Olympic Women's Fast Pitch Softball competitions. For more information or a schedule of games, call (706) 571 8866.

Children's imaginations are put to the test at the **Confederate Naval Museum** (101 Fourth Avenue), the only such museum in existence. There's little left of the hulls of the Confederate ironclad *Jackson* and the gunboat *Chattahoochee*, but sketches will let youngsters see what the boats looked like more than 125 years ago. Other relics from the Confederate navy are exhibited at the museum. The museum is open Tuesday through Saturday from 10:00 A.M. to 5:00 P.M. and Sunday from 1:00 to 5:00 P.M. Call (706) 327–9798.

Young people can trace the evolution of the U.S. infantry from the French and Indian War to the present at Fort Benning's **National Infantry Museum** on Baltzell Avenue. Among the special exhibits is the largest and most complete collection of military and small arms in the United States, artifacts from each of America's military involvements from the French and Indian War to Desert Storm, military documents signed by each of America's presidents, silver presentation pieces, military band instruments, captured enemy paraphernalia, and a tribute to General Omar Bradley. The museum is open Tuesday through Friday from 10:00 A.M. to 4:30 P.M. and weekends from 12:30 to 4:30 P.M. It is closed Thanksgiving, Christmas, and New Year's days. Call (706) 545–2958.

Columbus has a secret that you might miss if you're not careful: the striking **Riverfront/Riverwalk** along the bluffs and banks of the Chattahoochee River. A perfect place to walk, jog, or relax, the brick-paved promenade is embellished with ironwork, historical markers, sculptures, and benches.

An exhibit of thousands of lunch boxes dating back to 1900 is sure to tickle any child's fancy at the **South 106 Lunch Box and Collectibles Museum** at 1236 Broadway. When they've finished laughing over the old lunch pails, they can peruse the old radios, photography, advertising artwork, and Columbus memorabilia. The museum is open Monday through Friday by appointment. To find out more, call (706) 596–5400.

Watching how a newspaper is published or how some of our food items get to the grocery store shelves can be real eye openers for youngsters. Several of Columbus's industries offer plant tours. Children fourth grade level and above can see complete newspaper production at the Columbus *Ledger-Enquirer* at 17 West Twelfth Street. Free tours are given Tuesday and Thursday or by appointment. Call (706) 324–5526. Children at least nine years old can watch snack cake production at **Dolly Madison** at 1969 Victory Drive. Free tours are given Fridays at 10:30 A.M. or by appointment. Call (706) 324–6616. The kids can observe as the production lines turn out candy, snacks, cookies, and crackers at **Tom's Foods** at 900 Eighth Street. Tours are given on Tuesdays at 9:30 A.M. and 10:30 A.M. by appointment only. Call (706) 323–2721.

BUENA VISTA

Tiny Buena Vista, which bills itself as "America's Front Porch," offers fans of country music a special treat at the **National Country Music Museum** on the square. Stage clothing, musical instruments, cars, and other personal items from more than 100 stars are on display The museum is open by appointment. Call (800) 531–0677.

Youngsters won't know where to look first as they feast their eyes on bizarre and brilliantly painted walls, pagodas, totems, and other outdoor sculptures at **Pasaquan**, County 78 off State 137, the four-acre complex created by the late folk artist Eddie Owens Martin. Guided tours are available Saturday from 9:00 A.M. to 5:00 P.M. and Sunday from 1:00 to 5:00 P.M. or by appointment. Call (912) 649–9444.

Family members can simply tap their toes as they listen or kick up their heels as they dance to the best in country music performed by Nashville headliners and local artists one weekend a month at the **Silver Moon Music Barn** (State 41), one of the largest indoor showplaces in the Southeast. For a schedule of events or ticket information, call (800) 531–0677.

There's plenty of heart-pounding excitement to watch at the **Silver Moon Stampede Arena**, State 41. You can go back again and again to catch rodeos, horse shows, tractor pulls, and other electrifying events. To check on schedules of events and ticket information, call (800) 531–0677.

ANDERSONVILLE

Take a trip back in time to see what life was like in a Civil War prison camp at the **Andersonville National Historic Site** (State 49), the location of an infamous Civil War prison for captured Union soldiers. Almost 13,000 Northern soldiers died and are buried there. During living history presentations, the inhuman conditions under which the prisoners lived as well as some of the cruel tactics used to keep them subdued are demonstrated. At the visitor center see exhibits about Andersonville and other Civil War prisons. A brochure and audiotape are available for a self-guided tour of the site. The Prisoner of War Museum traces American wars from the Revolution to Vietnam. The site is open daily from 8:00 A.M. to 5:00 P.M. year-round and 8:00 A.M. to 7:00 P.M. on Memorial Day when the cemetery is awash in American flags placed on each grave. For more information, call (912) 924–0343.

Before the day is over, you'll want to stop in at the **Drummer Boy Civil War Museum**, located in the old railway depot, which also serves as the town's welcome center, to peruse authentic documents, guns, swords, flags, uniforms, and other Civil War relics. The museum is open Tuesday through Saturday from 10:00 A.M. to 4:00 P.M. from spring through fall. The welcome center is open daily from 9:00 A.M. to 5:00 P.M. except Christmas Day. Call (912) 924–2558.

The highlight of the year in the tiny village is the **Andersonville Historic Fair**, which is so popular it is held twice—once in May and again in October. Parents may be more interested in the wares of the 200 antique dealers, the Civil War collectibles, or the arts and crafts, but the whole family—especially the children—are thrilled by the Civil War reenactments and the demonstrations of old-time crafts by skilled artisans. For more information and the exact dates of the fair, call (912) 924–2558.

Escape into the past with a visit to **Trebor Plantation** on State 49. Built in 1833, the plantation was the home of Robert Hughes, a Confederate chaplain who attempted to serve the spiritual needs of the Union prisoners of war at Andersonville prison. The Greek Revival house with Edwardian adaptations was immortalized in McKinley Kantor's Pulitzer Prize–winning book *Andersonville*. Plantation dependencies (outbuildings) dot the grounds, which you may tour separately or in conjunction with the house. The plantation is open daily except Tuesday from 10:00 A.M. to 5:00 P.M. It is closed on Thanksgiving, Christmas Eve, Christmas Day, and New Year's Day. Call (912) 924–6886 for more information.

VIENNA

The smoky smell of barbecue fills the air during October's week-long **Big Pig Jig,** Georgia's annual Barbecue Cooking Championship. Listed as one of the Top Twenty Events in the Southeast by the Southeast Tourism Society and as one of America's Top 100 Events by the National Tour Bus Association, the festival features pageants, a parade, arts and crafts, a 5K Hog Run, hog calling, livestock shows, carnival rides, and four nights of stage shows. To find out the exact dates and more about the festival, call (912) 268–8275.

Ellis Brothers Pecans at exit 36 on I–75 offers tours of its pecan processing plant and confectionery during the fall season. Of course, you can purchase delicious pecan goodies there. The outlet is open Monday through Friday from 8:00 A.M. to 7:00 P.M. Call (912) 268-9041.

Take a trip back in time at the Andersonville Civil War Reenactment to see what life was like in a Civil War Camp.

LUMPKIN

Transport yourself back to stagecoach days and see how travelers fared at overnight stops by visiting the **Bedingfield Inn,** located on the courthouse square. Now a museum, the circa 1836 structure served as a stagecoach inn and family residence. Depending on the price they paid, overnight guests could get a private room, share a bed with several other travelers in the common room, or sleep on the floor. The inn is furnished with pieces appropriate to the period. Don't leave without picking up a brochure for the **Stagecoach Trail,** a driving tour past twenty-three pre–1850 homes. The museum is open daily from 1:30 to 5:00 P.M. or by appointment. Call (912) 838–6310.

If you want to look back at an old small-town apothecary shop, take the family to visit **Dr. Hatchett's Drug Store Museum** on Main Street on the square. Considered one of the finest turn-of-the-century drug store museum collections in the South, the museum contains all the furnishings and fixtures of an apothecary shop, as well as medicine bottles, antique packaging, a working soda fountain, and an ice cream parlor. The museum is open daily from 11:00 A.M. to 7:00 P.M. Call (912) 838–6924.

Continue your journey into yesteryear with a stop at **The Singer Co.** at 201 Main Street on the square. Georgia's oldest hardware store, this emporium has been operated by members of the same family since 1838. Children can spend hours examining the memorabilia, which includes ledgers and journals from the early 1800s, original fixtures, and rolling ladders. The store is open Monday through Saturday from 9:00 A.M. to 6:00 P.M. and Sunday from 1:00 to 5:00 P.M. Call (912) 838–4300.

You'll be experiencing living history at its best in an 1850s Georgia town at **Westville Village** on Martin Luther King Boulevard. Entirely constructed of buildings from the mid-1800s that have been relocated to this spot, the re-created hamlet contains houses that range from log cabins to elegant town homes, as well as churches, a school, stores, a blacksmith shop, a cotton gin, and numerous farm buildings. The costumed Westville "residents" go about their daily duties right before your eyes—cooking, gardening, basket weaving, pottery making, rake making, black smithing, shoe making, and much more. Among the special events held at Westville each year, the two most significant are the autumn Fair of 1850 and the Christmas festivities. During the fall fair demonstrators show fascinated youngsters how to grind corn and make syrup as well as how the cotton gin operates. The village is open from 10:00 A.M. to 5:00 P.M. Monday through Saturday and Sunday from 1:00 to 5:00 P.M. except Thanksgiving, Christmas, and New Year's days. To find out more about Westville or to get a schedule of activities, call (912) 838–6310.

Travel down old country roads to see an ecological phenomenon at **Providence Canyon State Conservation Park** on State 39C. The youngsters can hardly believe that little more than 100 years of erosion have created the spectacular 150-foot-deep gorge known as Georgia's Little Grand Canyon. Even more stunning than the depth and the varicolored canyon walls are the phantasmagorical formations resembling aboveground stalagmites that punctuate the chasm. Without expending much physical effort you can get several striking views of the formations and canyon walls from rim overlooks. Make sure you have plenty of film, because the varicolored walls present an ever-changing painting as different qualities of light strike them. The more energetic can hike down into the canyon by way of several hiking trails. Providence Canyon is also noted for having the largest concentration of wildflowers in the state and a large collection of the orange plumleaf or prunifolia azaleas that grow only within the 100-mile area. In addition, the park offers an interpretive center and picnicking facilities. One of Georgia's Seven Natural Wonders, the park is open from 7:00 A.M. to 6:00 P.M. between September 15 and April 14 and from 7:00 A.M. to 9:00 P.M. between April 15 and September 14. For more information, call (912) 838–6202.

OMAHA

You can create a memorable trip for the family by visiting **Florence Marina State Park** (State 39C) on **Lake Walter F. George**. In addition to the water sports available on the lake, you'll find a boat ramp and dock, rental fishing boats, a swimming pool, tennis courts, and picnicking facilities. Your choice of accommodations runs from campsites to cottages. The park is open from 7:00 A.M. to 10:00 P.M. Call (912) 838–6870 to learn more about the park. Within Florence Marina State Park, the **Kirbo Interpretive Center** houses nature exhibits and artifacts from the former pioneer town of Florence as well as relics from local Native American history that stretches back to the Paleo–Indian period. Guided walking tours are provided to eight Rood Creek Indian Mounds constructed between A.D. 900 and 1540. Ranging in size from 3-foot circular mounds to 25-foot pentagonal pyramids, five of the mounds are located around what was a central plaza surrounded by a moat. The museum center is open daily from 8:00 A.M. to 5:00 P.M. For more information about the museum, call (912) 838–4706.

FORT GAINES

Lake Walter F. George is a great place to start a family adventure. The 48,000-acre lake offers 640 miles of shoreline and twenty-three public access areas. Make sure to save time to visit the lake's **Lock and Dam**, the second highest lock east of the Mississippi. See a film about the lake and examine the exhibits in the interpretive center. In the winter the center is open from 8:00 A.M. to 4:30 P.M. Monday through Friday. From April 1 through October 1, it is open from 9:30 A.M. to 6:00 P.M. daily. Call (912) 768–2516.

An excellent place to stay on Lake Walter F. George is **George T. Bagby State Park and Lodge** on State 39. In addition to camp sites—many of them lakefront—this park boasts several cottages and a thirty-room lodge with a restaurant featuring family dining with a lakeside view. Among the adventures in which active family members might want to participate are fishing, tennis, swimming at the beach or pool, or hiking. The park provides a boat ramp and dock, as well as rentals of fishing boats, canoes, and pedal boats. The park is open daily from 7:00 A.M. to 10:00 P.M. Call (912) 768–2571.

For even more family fun, visit the **Frontier Village**, located on a scenic bluff overlooking the Chattahoochee River. Established in 1814 to protect settlers from Indian attacks, it also served as a Confederate fort in 1863 as the Confederacy tried to keep the Union from getting up the Chattahoochee River to the vital town of Columbus. See a one-third-actual-size replica of the fort as well as several authentic log cabins and the hand-carved 18-foot-tall oak totem by sculptor Otis Micco. The gigantic figure of an Indian brave's head, it is the only memorial to the Creek Indians ever erected in the old Creek Nation. Even farther up the hill is the **Outpost Replica**, off State 39, a reconstruction of an 1816–1830 fort used to protect settlers from attacks by Creek and Seminole Indians. Both the village and the outpost are open daily from 7:00 A.M. to 10:00 P.M. Call (912) 768–2934.

BLAKELY

Another of Georgia's picturesque covered bridges is the **Coheelee Creek Covered Bridge** at State 62 and Old River Road. Built in 1891, the bridge is 90 feet long and two spans wide. Pack a picnic and enjoy your meal in the adjacent picnic area.

Kolomoki Mounds State Park on State 39 is a must-see attraction on the agenda of any family traveling in southwest Georgia. The focal point of the park is a collection of seven large mounds from the Mississippian culture of Native Americans who flourished here more than 1,000 years ago. The principal mound is one of the largest temple mounds east of the Mississippi. A visit to the interpretive center allows you not only an opportunity to examine artifacts unearthed from the mounds, but permits access to a partially excavated mound with actual artifacts and replicas of skeletons in place where they were found. Offering camping, picnicking, a lake, a boat ramp and dock, fishing boat rentals, fishing, a swimming pool, and nature trails, the park is open daily from 7:00 A.M. to 10:00 P.M.; the interpretive center is open from 9:00 A.M. to 5:00 P.M. Tuesday through Saturday and from 2:00 to 5:30 P.M. on Sunday. To find out more, call (912) 723–5296.

ALBANY

The family can take a walk on the wild side at the **Chehaw Wild Animal Park** located within the grounds of **Chehaw Park** on Philema Road/State 91. Throughout the 100 acre tree-shaded wildlife preserve, trails and elevated walkways allow family members to see elk, ostriches, llamas, deer, zebras, elephants, buffalo, and other exotic visitors to Georgia. The petting zoo provides children with an opportunity to get close to some of the gentler creatures. A miniature train ride chugs around the park. The zoo is open from 9:00 A.M. to 6:00 P.M. daily. Chehaw Park itself is a 700 acre recreational park that includes play areas; jogging, bicycle, and nature trails; and campgrounds. In addition, it is the home of the **Chehaw National Indian Festival** held the third Saturday in May. A major Indian cultural event in the Southeast, the festival features traditional dancers, skills demonstrations, crafts, and storytelling. The overall park is open daily from 9:00 A.M. to dusk. It is closed Mondays and Christmas Day. For more information about the park or the zoo, call (912) 430–5275.

On a hot summer day, there's no better place for an inexpensive family outing than **Radium Springs and Casino** at 2500 Radium Springs Road. Another of the Seven Natural Wonders of Georgia, Radium Springs is the state's largest natural spring. It might take a moment or two to let your body adjust to the bone-chilling water that remains at 68 degrees year-round, but once you've adjusted, the rest of the day will be blissful. Confined in an irregularly shaped lagoon, the pool is surrounded by a beach and grassy shaded areas. An island in the middle of the spring tempts the energetic to swim over to it. Concerts are offered on the lawn during the summer months. Today the imposing 1926 casino operates as a restaurant that serves a Friday night buffet and Sunday brunch. The springs are open daily from 10:00 A.M. to 7:00 P.M. for swimming from Memorial Day to Labor Day. Call (912) 889–0244.

As you leave Radium Springs, stop at Radium Springs Road and Sands Drive. Youngsters won't believe what they're seeing when they take a gander at the gigantic **Sand Dunes** looming up right before their eyes. According to experts these fossil dunes were at the edge of the Gulf of Mexico one million years ago. Today no waves lap the dunes because the Gulf is 100 miles away.

The best way to become acquainted with Albany's history is to visit the **Thronateeska Heritage Museum of History and Science** at 100 Roosevelt in a historic railroad depot. Among the indoor exhibits, youngsters can inspect a giant grizzly bear, a collection of Indian artifacts, and changing historical exhibits. Outside they can survey antique automobiles and carriages, and an old train, as well as a model train exhibit housed in a baggage car. The museum is open Monday through Friday from noon to 5:00 P.M. and Saturday from 2:00 to 5:00 P.M. In an old Railway Express building adjacent to the depot, the complex also offers a science center and a planetarium. At the **Science Discovery Center** children can participate in such hands-on activities as forecasting the weather or capturing lightning. Programs are given at 10:00 A.M. and 2:00 P.M. during the summer months and at 3:30 P.M. during the school year. Situated in the same building, the **Wetherbee Planetarium**, the only planetarium in southwest Georgia, offers changing shows on Saturdays at noon, 1:00 P.M., and 3:00 P.M. For information on any of these attractions, call (912) 432–6955.

TIFTON

It's not a substitute for seeing exotic animals live and in person, but young ones can see a series of wondrous animals in the natural history exhibit at **Abraham Baldwin College** on Davis Road and Baldwin Drive. Among the exhibited creatures are sixty-two African animals as well as examples of North American mammals. In addition, the museum features an outstanding display of Masai tribal art. See the animals and the art from 9:00 A.M. to 5:00 P.M. on weekdays. To find out more, call (912) 386–3260.

For a cool treat on a hot day, spend some time on the beach and hurtling down the water slides at the **Crystal Beach and Water Park** on

State 125. The water park is open daily from 9:00 A.M. to 5:00 P.M. between Memorial Day and Labor Day. From April 1 through Memorial Day, the park is open on Saturday and Sunday from 9:00 A.M. to 5:00 P.M. For more information, call (912) 831–4655 or 382–9800.

Do your children want to know about life in turn-of-the-century Georgia? If so, they can leave the modern world behind and get a feel for life in that era at the **Georgia Agrirama Living History Center** at I–75 and Eighth Street. Depicting the period from 1870 to 1890, the rural village has been created by relocating thirty-five restored nineteenth-century buildings from around Georgia, including several farmsteads; town homes; a church; a school; commercial buildings such as a newspaper office, a feed and seed store, and an apothecary shop; a railroad depot; and an industrial complex that includes a sawmill, a gristmill, a cooper's, a blacksmith shop, and a turpentine still. A steam locomotive pulls wooden open-air cars around the complex. Costumed guides set newspaper type, saw lumber, sell lemonade, and carry out other chores from the late 1800s. Special events at the Agrirama include the County Fair of 1896 in May, the November cane-grinding parties, and the **1890s Victorian Christmas Celebration.** At the **Wiregrass Opry,** performed from 7:00 to 10:00 P.M. on Saturday evenings from April through October, you can clap your hands and tap your feet to the rhythms of country, bluegrass, and gospel music. In addition, there may be clogging or theatrical performances. The village is open Tuesday through Saturday from 9:00 A.M. to 5:00 P.M. and Sunday from 12:30 to 5:00 P.M. It is closed Mondays, New Year's Day, Thanksgiving Day, and the three days prior to and including Christmas Day. To learn more about the Agrirama, call (912) 386–3344.

THOMASVILLE

In the waning years of the nineteenth century, Thomasville enjoyed a golden age as wealthy northerners discovered that the area made an attractive place to spend the winter. The privileged classes were particularly drawn to the Plantation Trace by the abundance of wild game for hunting, but they built magnificent vacation homes and developed a rich cultural life there as well. Although the extension of the railroads into Florida and the general vagaries of the rich and famous eventually decreed that

Thomasville lost out to more trendy destinations, the city still has much to offer. Known as the Rose City because of its profusion of 20,000 bushes of the fragrant blossoms, Thomasville is located in the center of the biggest concentration of still-operating plantations in America.

Invite your youngsters to make believe that they have been transported to the opulent times enjoyed by Thomasville's winter visitors at the turn of the century by visiting **Pebble Hill Plantation** on US 319S. The present mansion, built in the 1930s to replace an earlier house that burned, is filled with antique furnishings, sporting art, crystal, china, and sterling silver, as well as an extensive collection of Indian artifacts. Please note that children younger than six are not admitted to the house. That's not to say, however, that young children will be left out or disappointed. The grounds are a destination in themselves. Tour the stables and other outbuildings, which include the kennels, a school, an infirmary, and other structures important to running a plantation. Youngsters particularly enjoy the garage filled with vintage cars and carriages and are delighted with a replica of Noah's Ark. The grounds are open Tuesday through Saturday from 10:00 A.M. to 5:00 P.M. and Sunday from 1:00 to 5:00 P.M. Guided tours of the house are conducted during those hours. Beginning the day after Labor Day, the plantation is closed for the remainder of September. Call (912) 226–2344 for more information.

You and the children can travel back to yesteryear at the **Thomas County Historical Museum** at 725 North Dawson, where the numerous exhibits include memorabilia from the hotel era of the late 1800s, artifacts from the area's many plantations, a ladies' dress collection of the period 1820 to 1940, a turn-of-the-century bowling alley, and several antique automobiles. The museum is open daily from 2:00 to 5:00 P.M. For more information, call (912) 226–0588.

If your family has ever wanted to stay at a Tara-like plantation, **Susina Plantation** on Meridian Road is the answer to your dream. The exterior of the Greek Revival mansion, built in 1841, features a pillared front shaded by massive Spanish-moss-laden live oaks. Scarlett would be right at home in the interior, which is characterized by high ceilings, intricate carvings, and ornate plasterwork and enhanced with antique furnishings and decorative fireplaces. Some guest accommodations boast a private veranda or a screened-in porch. Both a full Southern breakfast and a five-course gourmet dinner are included in the nightly rate. Although Susina Plantation makes an excellent base from which to explore Thomasville and the Plantation Trace, you could spend your entire vacation without leaving the property. Among the amenities that will keep any child occupied are a lighted tennis court, a swimming pool, a stocked fishing pond, and a jogging trail. For information or reservations, call (912) 377–9644.

Your youngsters can become better acquainted with wildlife at the **Birdsong Nature Center** at 2106 Meridian Road. Originally Birdsong Plantation, the land was worked from the 1850s to the 1930s by one family. Since 1938 it has been a haven for wildlife—a 565-acre nature sanctuary of habitat and wildlife diversity. The Bird Window allows children to observe birds without frightening them. At the Listening Place, if the kids are quiet and listen carefully, they'll hear a symphony of bird calls. In addition, the center features a butterfly garden and nature trails. The nature center is open Wednesday and Friday from 9:00 A.M. to noon, Saturday from 9:00 A.M. to 2:00 P.M., and Sunday from 1:00 to 5:00 P.M. Guided tours are arranged by appointment. Call (912) 377–4408.

BAINBRIDGE

Taking advantage of a 600-acre lake created by impounding the Flint River as it flows right through the heart of Bainbridge, the busy **Earl May Boat Basin Park** on West Shortwell Street provides adventure for all ages. Boat docks, a marina, a beach, tennis courts, twelve camping sites, fishing, picnicking, a steam engine museum, and a playground all attract fun-loving families. To find out more, call the Bainbridge–Decatur County chamber of commerce at (912) 246–4774.

For anglers in the family, spend a day or more on **Lake Seminole**, located at the confluence of the Chattahoochee and Flint rivers off State 97. The 37,500-acre lake, renowned for its superb freshwater fishing, is considered to be one of the best bass fishing lakes in the country, where fishermen can try their luck for lunker largemouth, hybrid, striped, and white bass. Twenty public-access points provide opportunities for camping, picnicking, boating, waterskiing, and swimming. To learn more about what the lake offers, call (912) 662–2001.

Wingate's Bass Island Campground (139 Wingate Road off State 310N) is for the family seeking adventure and diversity. Most families go to Wingate's for the wide variety of fishing experiences. Campers like the fact that every site at the year-round campground, located at Hutchinson Ferry Landing on Lake Seminole, boasts a lake view. If your family doesn't particularly like to camp, the complex offers sixteen motel rooms in Lunker Lodge. Other amenities include washers and dryers, a fishing pier, a playground, and a store that carries bait and tackle, gas, ice, and groceries. Even those who don't stay at Wingate's come from miles around to enjoy the day's fresh catch and Georgia barbecue in the unassuming atmosphere of the casual restaurant. Last, but not least, Wingate's offers a summer camp for boys. To find out more about any of the facilities at Wingate's, call (912) 246–0658.

COLQUITT

Family members may not be impressed that Colquitt is the **Mayhaw Jelly Capital** of Georgia if they don't know what a mayhaw is. Actually the mayhaw berry is a cranberry-sized fruit found in the swamps and bogs of southwest Georgia, and the jelly made from it is delicious. During the annual April **Mayhaw Festival**, you can see where the jelly is made, taste it for yourself, and shop for delicious mayhaw products. If you can't make it to the festival, you can purchase the jelly at the local grocery store where it is made. For information and dates for the festival, call (912) 758–2400.

Music and humor will draw you into the lives of early southwest Georgians at **Swamp Gravy Gospel**, a local folk history play based on the oral history recollections of long-time residents. Designated as a Cultural Olympiad event for the 1996 Summer Olympic Games, the play is a sequel to **Swamp Gravy Sketches**, so if your family has seen the first installment, they'll surely want to see the second. Call the chamber of commerce for a schedule of the spring and fall performances, (912) 758–2400.

Don't leave town without letting the children see the **Tribute to the American Indian**, US 27, the 23-foot-tall head of an Indian brave carved by Hungarian sculptor Peter Toth.

DONALSONVILLE

A great family playground, **Seminole State Park** on State 39 offers tent and trailer sites, pioneer camping, cottages, a beach, a boat ramp and dock, fishing, and waterskiing. The park, however, is best known as the location of the **Gopher Tortoise Nature Trail**, which wends its way through the habitat of Georgia's only native tortoise. The park is open daily from 7:00 A.M. to 10:00 P.M. Call (912) 861–3137 to learn more.

GENERAL INDEX

Abraham Baldwin College, 150
Adairsville, 79
Albany, 140
Allatoona Dam, 77
Alliance Children's Theater, 90
Alpharetta, 80
Alpine Amusement Park, 51
Altamaha River, 114
American Adventures, 85
Amicalola Falls, 62
Amicalola River Rafting Outpost, 62
Andersonville, 143
Andersonville National Historic Site, 143
Andy's Trout Farm, 31
Appalachian Outfitters, 59
Athens, 1
Atlanta Braves, 97
Atlanta Falcons, 97
Atlanta Hawks, 97
Atlanta Heritage Row, 91
Atlanta Knights, 97
Atlanta Metro, 89
Atlanta Motor Speedway, 14
Atlanta Symphony Orchestra, 90
Atlanta Thunder, 97
Auchumpkee Covered Bridge, 141
Augusta, 43
Augusta Canal, 42
Augusta Trolley, 42

B & H Orchards, 13
BabyLand Beneral Hospital, 49
Bainbridge, 153
Barnesville, 14
Bartow History Center, 69
Baxley, 114
Berry College, 77
Big Peach Monument, 24
Big Red Oak Creek Bridge, 134
Birdsong Nature Center, 153
Blairsville, 57
Blakely, 148
Bloddy Marsh Battle Site, 117
Blue Bird Body Company, 22
Br'er Rabbit Statue, 10
Braille Trail, 121
Braselton, 46
Brasstown Bald Mountain, 57
Brenau College, 46

Brunswick, 107
Buena Vista, 143
Burkett's Ferry, 114
Burt's Pumpkin Farm, 62

Cabbage Patch Kids, 49
Cainesville, 46
Calhoun, 73
Capitol, 95
Carnesville, 36
Carriage Tours of Savannah, 106
Carter's Dam, 71
Carter's Lake Marina and Resort, 71
Cartersville, 77
Cartersworth, 62
Cave Spring, 77
Cecil B. Day Butterfly Center, 134
Center for Puppetry Arts, 91
Center of the World, 37
Central of Georgia Railroad Roundhouse
    Complex, 105
Chappell's Mill, 25
Chateau Elan Winery and Resort, 46
Chatsworth, 71
Chattahoochee Nature Center, 83
Chattahoochee Stables, 52
Chauncey, 26
Chesser Island Homestead, 126
Chickamauga and Chattanooga National
    Military Park, 70
City Exchange Bell, 106
Clarkesville, 48
Claxton, 104
Claxton Fruitcake Company, 104
Clayton, 32
Cleveland, 49
Clinton, 19
Cloister Hotel, The, 119
CNN Center, 95
Coast Guard Station, 118
Coheelee Creek Covered Bridge, 148
Colquitt, 154
Columbus, 141
Columbus Redstixx Baseball Team, 141
Commerce, 45
Concord Bridge, 86
Confederate Monument, 43
Confederate Powder Works, 43
Consolidated Mines, 60

ACTIVITIES INDEX

Lakes

Family Programs

Summer Family Adventure Program, 135
Summer Fun for Families, 123
Summer Family Festival, 121

Trails

Appalachian Trail, 62
Bartram Trail, 32
Blue and Gray Trail, 6
Boarding House Trail, 11
Canal Diggers Trail, 126
Chieftains Trail, 67
Deer Stand Trail, 126
Earth Day Nature Trail, 116
Gopher Tortoise Nature Trail, 155
Indian Mounds Trail 11
Peckerwood Trail, 126
Pine Mountain Trail, 137
Stagecoach Trail, 145

Welcome Centers

Church-Waddel-Brumby House/Welcome
    Center, 3,
Eagle Tavern Welcome Center, 4
Macon-Bibb County Convention and
    Visitors Bureau/Welcome Center, 19
Rabun County Welcome Center, 32
Rome Welcome Center, 75–76
Savannah Visitor Center, 105
Terrora and Visitors Center, 35
Vidalia Welcome Center, 104
Welcome Centers for Brunswick and the
    Golden Isles, 117
Cotton Exchange Welcome Center and
    Museum, 41

ABOUT THE AUTHORS

Carol and Dan Thalimer have been writing about travel for the last eight years. In addition to the hundreds of articles they have written for newspapers and magazines nationwide, they have contributed to numerous guides for Birnbaum, Fodor's, and Frommer's and have compiled several travel guides of their own, including *Quick Escapes from Atlanta* (The Globe Pequot Press, 1996). Their other travel guides include *Georgia Outdoor Activity Guide, Georgia B & Bs,* and *Country Roads of Georgia.*